DORSET
TRACTION

Mark Jamieson

AMBERLEY

About the Author

Coming from a family with a working railway background, it was inevitable that I would develop 'the bug'. A lifelong railway enthusiast from a relatively early age, I grew up within a stone's throw of the now closed section of railway that ran from Poole to Broadstone and on towards Wimborne or Blandford Forum – not a million miles from the present Poole to Hamworthy main line.

My dad was a keen amateur photographer and I would often look through his photography magazines. From this casual browsing, an interest was born.

However, it was Ivo Peters' inspirational book *Railway Elegance* from the mid-1980s that really kick-started my creative interest, and it was to become a major influence on my photographic style in the years to come.

Being born and bred in Dorset, and with a love of the countryside, most of my photographs are principally taken around my home county and the surrounding counties, with an emphasis on trying to capture the best shots possible as I try to strive for excellence, not perfection.

Front cover: The signaller's view from the signal box at Dorchester South on 7 April 2017 as No. 444017 departs with 1W58, the 11:20 Weymouth to Waterloo SWT service.

Rear cover: Lots of activity at Dorchester West on 10 May 2017 as No. 150266 stands with 2E26, the 15:08 Weymouth to Gloucester GWR service.

First published 2017

Amberley Publishing
The Hill, Stroud
Gloucestershire, GL5 4EP

www.amberley-books.com

Copyright © Mark Jamieson, 2017

The right of Mark Jamieson to be identified as the Author of this work has been asserted in accordance with the Copyrights, Designs and Patents Act 1988.

ISBN 978 1 4456 7167 3 (print)
ISBN 978 1 4456 7168 0 (ebook)

British Library Cataloguing in Publication Data.
A catalogue record for this book is available from the British Library.

Origination by Amberley Publishing.
Printed in the UK.

Introduction

Dorset, where the South Coast meets the West Country. From golden sandy beaches to rolling hills, delightful seaside towns and idyllic country villages, Dorset has long been a popular destination for visitors.

Just out of the reach of the majority of commuters to London, and bypassed by many heading to Devon or Cornwall for their much-needed holiday break, this is a county still very much untouched by massive development, although times are changing.

Known by the Romans as Durnovaria, the county town of Dorchester lies in a fairly central position within Dorset. Poole and Bournemouth lie to the east, Weymouth and Portland to the south, Bridport and Lyme Regis to the west, and towns like Gillingham and Sherborne lie to the north.

From castles like Corfe and Sherborne, historic homes such as Wolfeton House near Dorchester or Kingston Lacy near Wimborne, and with the Jurassic Coast, rich in prehistoric fossils with its world-famous Lulworth Cove, Dorset is a county steeped in history and heritage.

Unlike the more industrious regions of the Midlands or the North, Dorset is principally a rural county and has very little in the way of heavy industry – so much so that it is unusual insomuch that it has no motorway and very few dual-carriageway roads.

The county lends itself to agriculture but is also a popular destination for visitors and those wishing to relocate for work. Until 1 April 1974, the biggest town was Poole. However, under the Local Government Act 1972, the county's boundary was to change, with Bournemouth and Christchurch being transferred from Hampshire into Dorset, thereafter making Bournemouth its largest town.

Although not home to a vast railway network, several main lines cut through the county or terminate there. The most famous line to pass through the county was the long-closed Somerset & Dorset Joint Railway from Bath to Bournemouth via Blandford Forum.

Many other lines were also closed over the years, including the 'Old Road' main line to Dorchester from Brockenhurst via Ringwood, West Moors, Wimborne, Broadstone and Hamworthy. Also axed were the branch lines serving Lyme Regis, Bridport, Portland and Abbotsbury, as well as the Swanage branch from Wareham – all with their tracks being lifted.

The most recent closure has been the Weymouth Quay tramway, which saw its last train in 1999. Although the track remains in situ, is it likely to ever see a train again?

While threatened with heavy rationalisation, and indeed complete closure west of Bournemouth under the Serpell Report of 1983, the main line from Waterloo to Weymouth now enjoys its best service ever, with two trains per hour and an hourly service on Sundays. Likewise, the Waterloo to Exeter line that cuts through the north of the county also enjoys its best-ever service. Both of these lines are served by South West Trains, with – at the time of writing – the franchise due to be taken over by First Group/MTR Corporation during August 2017. The new Train Operating Company is to operate under the title of South Western Railway with a new silver and dark blue livery expected to be used.

Saved from extinction in the 1960s, but heavily rationalised under the Beeching cuts, the Great Western Railway-operated line from Yeovil to Weymouth has a sparse service. Likened to the Somerset & Dorset, this once double-track main line runs through some beautiful Dorset landscapes from the north to the south of the county via Maiden Newton and Dorchester.

Since the end of Southern steam in July 1967, and into the modern traction era, Dorset has been synonymous with the operation of Class 33/1s and 4TCs between Bournemouth and Weymouth, prior to the 1988 electrification west of Bournemouth. After twenty-one years of service, these now classic trains were replaced by the Class 442 'Wessex Electrics' until early 2007 when the Siemens-built Class 444 and 450 'Desiro' units took over, which have remained as the staple classes of traction in the south of the county.

The West of England route from Waterloo to Exeter lost its loco-hauled trains in June 1993 when the new BREL Derby-built Class 159s came into service. Twenty-four years later, they still work very reliably on the same line they were originally intended for.

Between Yeovil and Dorchester, the Great Western route has been dominated by multiple units since the end of steam, with the occasional loco-hauled extras appearing at peak times. Over recent years, the route has seen a summer Saturday service worked by an HST set from Bristol.

The county enjoys quite a few steam and diesel-hauled rail tours during the year, which are often bound for Bournemouth or Weymouth. However, since the private Swanage Railway reconnected its rebuilt line with the national network, Swanage and Corfe Castle have, not surprisingly, been a popular choice of destination for tour promoters.

Freight operations have never been that significant in Dorset, unlike hotspot areas of the country with heavy industry, and it has seen freight traffic steadily decline for many years. February 2014 saw the final freight train depart the county when the regular loaded-sand working from Wool to Neasden, operated by Freightliner Heavy Haul, made its final journey.

However, the county is starting to enjoy something of a freight revival in 2017, with a new flow of stone running to Hamworthy from the Mendip quarries. Likewise, the rail-served decommissioned nuclear power station at Winfrith is expected to export low-level waste by train.

The photographs chosen for this book represent some of the varied traction that Dorset has enjoyed over the years since the end of steam in 1967, as well as the landscapes through which the trains pass.

As a professional railwayman, I have been able to take photographs from the trackside within the boundary fence as I hold the relevant qualifications and permissions. Unless your work involves you going trackside as a railway employee or contractor and you hold the correct documentation and permissions, please remember that you must remain in a public place and be aware of your personal safety, and the safety of others, at all times.

All lineside photographs in this book were taken with authority. All belong to the author's own collection unless otherwise stated.

I must convey my heartfelt thanks to the following people who have assisted me in making this book possible: John Dedman; Mark Finch; Andrew P. M. Wright; Jim Boudreau; Steve McMullin; Nigel Nicholls; Glen Batten; Mark Pike; Colin Stone; Steve Clark; Nic Joynson; and of course the team at Amberley Publishing.

Mark Jamieson
Poole
May 2017

Currently the staple diet of the Waterloo to Bournemouth and Weymouth route, the Siemens Class 444 Desiro five-car electric multiple unit was introduced during 2004. Under a lovely spring morning sky on 24 March 2015, SouthWest Trains Desiro unit No. 444010 approaches Wool while working 1W54, the 09:20 Weymouth–Waterloo.

Having just emerged from the 819-yard-long Bincombe No. 1 Tunnel, First Great Western duo Nos 158763 and 150221 are about to pass through the much shorter 47-yard-long Bincombe No. 2 Tunnel while working 2O90, the 12:41 Worcester Foregate Street–Weymouth, on 21 June 2014. Evidence of a landslip some years previously can be seen to the lower left, with the ballast covering the cutting slope. In fact, the area has been prone to unstable earthworks since the days of the Great Western Railway.

The classic West of England route from Salisbury to Exeter weaves in and out of Dorset several times, and one such place is Sherborne in the north of the county. On 12 June 2010, three-car Class 159 unit No. 159008 approaches the north Dorset market town of Sherborne with a Waterloo-bound service.

The first station in Dorset on the Waterloo to Weymouth main line is Christchurch, and No. 450073 runs into the station on the evening of 30 June 2014 with 2B53, the Southampton–Poole stopping service. In essence, this is the rear portion of the 17:05 Waterloo–Weymouth service, which divides at Southampton; the front portion runs fast to Weymouth, and the rear portion then follows, stopping at all stations.

History is finally made on 13 June 2017. Operated by West Coast Railways under contract to the Swanage Railway, a two-year trial service commenced between Swanage and Wareham running five days a week with four return trips per day for a total of sixty days during 2017, which will rise to ninety running days during 2018. Passing Holme Lane, about a mile south of Worgret Junction, the Swanage Railway's main line-registered Class 33, No. 33012 *Lt Jenny Lewis RN* plus four coaches, with Class 37 No. 37518 to the rear, makes its way towards Wareham with 2Z24, the 16:23 Swanage–Wareham.

The former GWR line from Castle Cary to Weymouth cuts through some beautiful Dorset countryside and is served by Great Western Railway, formerly First Great Western. On 12 June 2010, with its four Mk 2 coaches in tow, No. 67016 heads south from Yetminster hauling 2O67, the 09:09 Bristol Temple Meads–Weymouth additional summer Saturday service.

ScotRail comes to Dorset in the shape of ex-works No. 47541 *The Queen Mother*, looking very smart in its recently applied ScotRail-branded InterCity livery. It is seen here at Bournemouth on 12 June 1986 with 1E63, the 10:40 Poole–Newcastle. The three-piece miniature snowplough completes the smart appearance, but any locomotive operating over a route with a conductor rail is required to have these in the 'raised position'.

Staple traction on the Bournemouth to Weymouth circuit for twenty-one years – between 1967 and 1988, following the end of steam on the Southern Region of British Rail – was the Class 33/1 and 4TC combination, which provided a cheaper alternative to full electrification beyond Branksome through to Weymouth. Electrification did eventually come during 1988, as can be seen by the newly laid conductor rails, but on 8 September 1987, some eight months before the full electric timetable was introduced, No. 33119 propels its 4TC set out of Upwey with 1W22, the 10:32 Weymouth–Waterloo. The signal to the left (former WA 397 signal) had recently been taken out of use as part of the re-signalling between Dorchester and Weymouth. It had yet to be recovered when Weymouth signal box finally closed on 19 September 1987 – hence the unusual sight of a signal facing away from the railway.

Somewhat off the beaten track is this Western Region Class 108 DMMU at Gillingham on 10 April 1988, running as 2Z70, the 11:36 Gillingham–Yeovil Junction. Weekend track renewals between Gillingham and Tisbury meant that Waterloo to Exeter services were diverted via Westbury, with a shuttle service in operation between Gillingham and Yeovil Junction. In the distance can be seen No. 47209 on an engineer's train just at the possession limits, with a trainload of recovered track panels. (Steve McMullin)

Poole Harbour is one of the largest natural harbours in the world, and within it is the tidal inland lake of Holes Bay. Opened on 1 June 1893, this embankment cut through Holes Bay to connect with the existing railway network at Hamworthy and Poole. On 13 January 2016, Network Rail No. 73138 leads 1Q43, the 08:32 Eastleigh Works–Eastleigh Works test train, via Weymouth. To the rear is GBRf-liveried classmate No. 73141 *Charlotte* as it crosses Holes Bay on the approach to Poole with the return working back to Eastleigh.

The uniquely liveried Bardon Aggregates blue Class 66 No. 66623 *Bill Bolsover* hurries past Winfrith Sidings, to the west of Wool, on 7 September 2013, working 6O49, the 10:23 Theale Lafarge Sidings–Wool running via Westbury, Salisbury, Eastleigh and Dorchester South. The siding leads into the former nuclear facility at Winfrith, which is currently in a state of decommissioning.

The first of four trains at Furzebrook in connection with earthworks renewals on 16 April 2015. Having been brought in by Colas Railfreight's Class 70 No.70809, running 6C18, the 06:56 Eastleigh Yard–Furzebrook Sidings, the train locomotive was duly removed to allow Swanage Railway Class 33 No. 33201 to draw the train down to the worksite for unloading. The Colas Class 70 would then go on the other end to return the train to Eastleigh. (Andrew P. M. Wright)

Well off the beaten track for a Class 56 is No. 56119, paired up with No. 33102, which is seen just after arrival at Weymouth with DC Tours' *Solent & Wessex Wanderer 2* working 1Z24, the 10:12 Waterloo–Weymouth, on 12 January 1992. A total of eight tours were run by this promoter, bringing a variety of unusual traction out of Waterloo to various destinations in the South West.

Departmental trip working 5B39, the 10:01 Wimbledon Park–Bournemouth depot, makes its way towards Christchurch formed of Nos 455739, 456005 and 456023. The entire fleet of twenty-four two-car Class 456 units had been transferred from Southern to SouthWest Trains during 2014. A couple of sets have been used in the Bournemouth area for testing purposes, but this was not their intended area of use once fully entered into service. Obviously, this pair are being tripped to Bournemouth for further testing on 17 February 2015.

On 8 May 1989, 4TC No. 8017, propelled by its Class 33/1 locomotive at the rear, runs into Gillingham working 1L07, the 12:10 Waterloo–Gillingham service. (Nic Joynson)

It could almost be the 1990s/2000s all over again at Bournemouth depot as Wessex Electric Class 442 No. 2418 stands on No. 7 Road. Alongside is Class 73 No. 73235 on No. 8 Road on 29 August 2016. They stand within the carriage cleaning shed, which dates back to about 1935 and hasn't changed a great deal over the years. The Wessex Electrics were introduced in 1988 upon completion of the Weymouth electrification. By January 2007, however, they were transferred to Southern upon the introduction of the Class 444 Desiro units.

With just a couple of weeks left before the introduction of the Class 442 Wessex Electrics on the Weymouth line, No. 33118 approaches Branksome with 1W21, the 10:32 Waterloo–Weymouth, on 22 April 1988.

Another first for the Swanage Railway was this visit by a Class 42 'Warship', courtesy of the East Lancs Railway Diesel Group at Bury. Looking quite at home, No. D832 *Onslaught* approaches Harmans Cross on 5 May 2016 during the railway's annual diesel gala while working a Swanage to Norden service.

Another impressive addition to the Swanage Railway 2016 diesel gala fleet was No. 20205, courtesy of the Class 20 Loco Society. Leading No. 20142, acting as a 'translator', seeing as No. 20205 is air-brake only and the coaching stock is vacuum-brake only, the immaculate Class 20 passes New Barn heading for Swanage with the 13:00 from Norden on 8 May 2016.

A mid-week ballast drop sees 'Dutch'-liveried Class 37 No. 37092 at Wyke, between Sherborne and Yeovil Junction, on 13 May 1992 with 7Z11, the 08:40 Exeter Riverside Yard–Gillingham (run-round) ballast train. The ballast train was formed of a plough van and Sealion and Dogfish wagons, which had been dropping ballast on the Up and Down lines between Sherborne and Yeovil Junction. (Steve McMullin)

A glorious afternoon as No. 58003 slowly makes its way through Poole on 5 August 1998 with 6V89, the 17:50 Hamworthy–Merehead Quarry stone empties. This traffic originally started during 1997 as a temporary flow for the construction of the A35 Puddletown bypass near Dorchester, but eventually became permanent traffic, such was the demand for aggregate in the construction industry. (Mark Finch)

8 June 2013 and it is a fine summer's day as a SouthWest Trains Class 444 Desiro passes the fields of rapeseed along Christchurch Bank at Stoney Cross, working a Waterloo to Weymouth service. This whole area has just been approved for a large housing development of 875 new houses between the railway and the A35.

A busy scene at the east end of Bournemouth station on 27 July 2008, with Platform 1 occupied by one of SouthWest Trains' Class 73s, No. 73235. Alongside, in Platform 2, is a Virgin Voyager unit, while to the left, in Platform 3, is a SouthWest Trains Class 444 Desiro unit. Platform 4 is an extension of Platform 3 that is located beyond the train shed. The long single Down platform is one of the longest platforms in the country, and is effectively divided into two.

With a trainload of new concrete sleepers, Colas Railfreight Class 70 No. 70809 passes East Burton – between Wool and Moreton – on 11 April 2015, working 6C05, the 14:02 Eastleigh Yard–Dorchester South, in connection with track renewals between Bincombe Tunnel and Upwey.

A fine summer's evening at Wareham as No. 444022 awaits time working 1W75, the 17:05 Waterloo–Weymouth on 15 August 2014. Situated just over half a mile from the town centre, the 1886-built station is largely unchanged since the days of steam and still retains many original features. To the left is the former Up bay platform, which at one stage was proposed for re-instatement, along with a run round facility for the use of Swanage Railway services. However, Network Rail have made passive provision for this area for any potential future use by the Swanage Railway.

The introduction of Class 47s to the Waterloo to Exeter route during 1991 allowed British Rail to withdraw the troublesome Class 50s. As a farewell gesture to the class, Network SouthEast organised a '50 Farewell Day' on Sunday 24 May 1992. Running into Gillingham with the 09:28 Exeter St Davids–Waterloo is No. D400/50050 *Fearless* leading No. 50007 *Sir Edward Elgar*, they would work it as far as Salisbury. (Glen Batten)

Looking right at home on the Swanage Railway is No. D5185 (TOPS number 25035) from the Great Central Railway, which is seen here on 9 May 2015 working the 13:20 Norden to Swanage service near Harmans Cross. The locomotive was obviously proving to be a popular choice and was loaded well. This was the final Class 25 to work a passenger train in BR service, when on 14 March 1987 it found itself on 1V09, the 07:09 Holyhead–Cardiff Central, after No. 47442 failed at Chester. The Class 25 took the train on to Crewe. It was withdrawn from BR service the following day.

History in the making on 25 March 1993 as the first Class 37 to traverse the Weymouth Quay tramway makes its way along Commercial Road and down towards Weymouth Quay. Top and tailing 4TC No. 410, with Class 73 No. 73109 *Battle of Britain* out of sight on the rear, is No. 37038, which is passing the Sailors Return pub. The Dutch-liveried Class 37 was being used to test the class on the tramway ahead of a planned summer service from Yeovil to Weymouth Quay during 1993.

Returning from Weymouth Quay, and equally as unusual as the Class 37, Class 73 No. 73109 *Battle of Britain* slowly negotiates its way past the boats alongside Weymouth Harbour while heading back to Weymouth station on 25 March 1993 with the Class 37 clearance test run.

A rare event in south Dorset these days – snow! Following an overnight covering, the landscape is transformed on the morning of 7 February 2009 as a Class 444 Desiro unit heads south from Dorchester, bound for Weymouth, almost blending in with its snowy surroundings!

On 11 June 2009, a Class 444 Desiro unit is seen north of Bincombe Tunnel heading towards Dorchester with a Weymouth to Waterloo service. Weymouth currently enjoys its best service ever to London, with two trains per hour during the day Monday to Saturday, and an hourly service on a Sunday.

Swanage Railway's resident Class 33/0, No. D6515 (TOPS number 33012) then named *Stan Symes*, accelerates away from Harmans Cross on 13 April 2008 with a freight working under an increasingly threatening sky.

A historic moment on 8 September 2002 sees Virgin Cross-Country Voyager unit No. 220018 head south away from Corfe Castle, bound for Swanage. Greeted by a huge crowd upon arrival at Swanage, the train would be named *Dorset Voyager* by two of Swanage Railway's long-serving volunteers, Moyra Cross and Stan Symes. (Andrew P. M. Wright)

The 'electric Deltic' of the South Western Main Line – the 3,000 hp Class 430 4-REP, comprising a fleet of fifteen units solely for use between Waterloo and Bournemouth. Here, No. 3013 stands in Middle Siding No. 1 at Bournemouth on 4 May 1985, with the front portion of 1W24, the 11:34 Weymouth–Waterloo, while No. 3014 stands in Middle Siding No. 2 prior to working the 13:00 semi-fast service to Waterloo. The final units soldiered on until withdrawal by September 1991, some three years after the line from Branksome to Weymouth was electrified and the brand-new BREL Derby-built Class 442 Wessex Electrics were fully introduced into service after a troublesome start.

A work-stained No. 33111 stands at Weymouth Quay with 4TC set No. 417 on 13 August 1985 before working 1W30, the 13:00 to Bournemouth/Waterloo. This locomotive would eventually go on to be preserved, and is currently based at Swanage Railway. Note the yellow British Rail permanent way crew van in the distance.

Class 50 No. 50009 *Conqueror* departs from Maiden Newton on 27 November 1986 with a test train from Weymouth consisting of Nos ADB977352, DB975982, DB977193 and track recording coach No. DW139. Presumably the Class 50 was selected thanks to its top speed of 100 mph, owing to some high speed testing requirements within the train's schedule. To the right is the track bed of the former Bridport branch, which was closed and lifted during 1975 – a late closure compared to many other lines around the country. (Steve McMullin)

The final week of 1993's summer timetable and No. 37421 is in trouble. Having just departed Weymouth station with the 11:35 Wednesdays-only trip to Weymouth Quay, the fire extinguishers in the cab were activated and discharged foam. The train was summarily halted and the locomotive duly declared a failure. Dutch-liveried No. 37191 was dispatched light engine from Westbury for the back working – 16:30 Weymouth–Bristol Temple Meads – and the pair are seen approaching Chetnole on 1 September 1993. No. 37421 would be detached at Westbury. (Steve McMullin)

Passing through Christchurch is No. 58010 with 6O39, the 09:24 Merehead Quarry to Hamworthy loaded stone train, on 9 March 1998. (Nic Joynson)

A smart-looking pair of Class 73s stand at Branksome on 4 August 1988 headed by No. 73202 *Royal Observer Corps*, with No. 73201 *Broadlands* tucked inside. The headcode '00' indicates this is an empty coaching stock move between Bournemouth depot and Poole/Bournemouth/Branksome, or vice-versa.

This is certainly off the beaten track for DRS. Passing Crockway Farm, near Maiden Newton, on 15 June 2010, is ex-works No. 37409 leading classmate No. 37423 *Spirit of the Lakes* on 2Z01, the 09:31 Waterloo–Southampton via Weymouth, with ex-Southern Region General Managers' Saloon No. TDB975025 *Caroline*.

One-time resident of the Swanage Railway Class 47 No. 47635 is seen here with a demonstration freight working, passing through Harmans Cross station on 12 April 2008. Originally one of the visiting locomotives at the railway's 2007 diesel gala, the former Colas-owned locomotive moved into private ownership and a new home at the railway, becoming a popular addition to the home fleet. However, by September 2008, it had worked its final train on the Swanage Railway before heading to a new home at Peak Rail.

Running into Dorchester South with 6O49, the 10:51 Neasden–Wool via Dorchester South empty hoppers, is Freightliner's No. 66510 on 9 May 2011. The train would shunt to the siding and split into two portions, with the wagons then being tripped up to Wool as two separate movements. Carrying sand quarried locally in the Moreton area and moved by road to the former MoD (Army) sidings at Wool, the wagons would then be conveyed fully loaded back to Neasden in north London. Formerly an EWS-operated flow that commenced regular operation during July 2000, EWS would lose the contract to Freightliner, who commenced operation on 3 April 2006. However, by 2011 the train was down to a once-weekly move, and would finish completely on 21 November 2014, when the final train ran. Thereafter, the working would transfer to GB Railfreight 'on paper', but has not run since it finished under Freightliner operations.

Spitfire Railtours' 'Routes & Branches III' tour on 22 October 2011, hauled by West Coast Railways Class 37 No. 37685 *Loch Arkaig*, arrives at Hamworthy Goods, running as 1Z37, the 07:09 Paddington–Portsmouth Harbour via Hamworthy Goods, Winchester and Botley. While several railtours have run here over the years, passenger working on this goods-only branch still presents an unusual sight. (Mark Pike)

After an absence of almost seven years, loco-hauled trains returned to Weymouth on a scheduled passenger service, albeit for one day only, on 3 June 2017. Unbranded DB red Class 67 No. 67010 gets away from Dorchester with an incredible eleven-coach set – made up of five ex-Anglia-liveried coaches, and six BR blue and grey coaches – working 1O72, the 09:06 Bristol Temple Meads–Weymouth summer Saturday service, which is usually worked by a HST set.

'Hastings' DEMU No. 1001 stands in the Reception Road at Poole on 8 August 2010, having arrived with 'The Andy Piper Memorial Tour' on 1Z80, the 07:05 Hastings–Poole via Waterloo. Of course, the 'Hampshire' DEMU units were no stranger to the area, having worked the Swanage branch after the end of BR steam on 4 September 1966 up until closure of the line on 3 January 1972, with servicing and fuelling being undertaken at Bournemouth.

Skirting the edge of Poole Harbour at Holton Lee on 28 September 2016, South West Trains No. 444029 passes with a Weymouth to Waterloo service. The bridge it is about to pass under once carried a long siding from the railway complex at the nearby Royal Naval Cordite Factory at Holton Heath to a jetty in Poole Harbour, but all lines were removed around 1961; the works eventually closed in the late 1990s.

The Poole Harbour Commissioners' 0-4-0 diesel shunter on Hamworthy Quay, Poole, with the first train load of steel billets, which had been transferred from ship to rail on 27 July 1999. Port of Poole had recently regained the contract from Newport Docks, and ironically the steel was destined for Allied Steel & Wire Cardiff (Cardiff Rod Mill). The traffic was, however, short-lived with the final train departing on 5 May 2000. Note the missing coupling, which required the locomotive to be lifted by crane and turned so as to maximise its operational use from one end only. (Colin Stone)

A pair of Class 159 units pass Lenthay Common on the approach to Sherborne on 3 August 2014, bound for Waterloo.

Seen from the rooftop signal box at Bournemouth, Dutch-liveried Class 73 No. 73129 *City of Winchester* passes on 8 August 1991 with a nuclear flask working from Winfrith. The station car park is probably best remembered as the location of the Bournemouth locomotive shed back in the days of steam. The shed closed with the end of steam in July 1967. The long Down platform at Bournemouth would offer a grandstand view to watch activities on- and off-shed, and the signal box was suitably positioned to supervise those moves.

A private charter in connection with a wedding on 16 July 1994, which was worked by No. 33206 and No. 33116 *Hertfordshire Railtours*. Formed of the Ocean Liner set, a dedicated set of stock operated by Network SouthEast's charter division, the special train is seen passing Oborne running as 1Z16, the 08:56 Waterloo–Sherborne. Originating from Waterloo with just No. 33116 *Hertfordshire Railtours*, a faulty headlight would necessitate an additional locomotive on the front at Woking, in the form of No. 33206. The private charter was to endure more drama as the pair of Class 33s then had problems with their couplings at Yeovil Junction, and No. 33109 *Captain Bill Smith RNR* was despatched to work the return working: 1Z17, the 19:05 Yeovil Junction–Waterloo via Westbury. (Steve McMullin)

As part of Armed Forces Day on 24 June 2017, GBRf Class 66 No. 66756 was named *Royal Corps of Signals* at Swanage by Major General John Crackett of the Royal Corps of Signals, based in Blandford Forum, and GB Railfreight's managing director John Smith. After the naming ceremony No. 66756 *Royal Corps of Signals* then worked an out-and-back trip from Swanage to Norden, before returning light engine to Eastleigh. Here it departs from the gloom at Corfe Castle, which only a couple of days earlier had been in the grip of a heatwave, with No. 33111 on the 14:40 Norden–Swanage. Alongside is the Swanage to Wareham shuttle service hauled by West Coast Railways Class 33 No. 33025 with No. 37518 trailing to the rear. (Andrew P. M. Wright)

The LCGB-promoted tour 'The Hampshireman' on 3 November 1968, running from Waterloo to Gosport, Fawley and Blandford Forum. Having arrived at Blandford Forum behind Class 74 No. E6108 (TOPS number 74008), which had brought the tour from Poole, it was now the turn of Class 47 No. D1986 (TOPS number 47284) to return to the tour out of Blandford Forum, where it is seen prior to departure. The Class 74 on the rear would be removed at Broadstone with the Class 47 continuing on to Waterloo via Bournemouth, Eastleigh, Alresford and Ascot. Passenger services by this stage on the Somerset & Dorset line had been withdrawn as of 7 March 1966 and Blandform Forum was reduced to goods traffic only, which would itself be withdrawn on 6 January 1969, with the S&D then finally being lifted. (Andrew P. M. Wright)

No. 66126 stands at Hamworthy Goods on 14 February 2006 with a trainload of contaminated oil waste, often referred to as 'mud oil'. The traffic commenced on 16 May 2002 but was sporadic, this being the final movement. Contaminated oil waste was a product from the local oil exploration based on Furzey Island, within Poole Harbour. The square metal containers that can be seen loaded on the train were taken to and from the island by barge to be filled with residue drilling lubricant (drilling 'mud'), or contaminated oil residue (dregs). They would be taken away for recycling or disposal within the four-wheel OBA wagons, destined for the Lowestoft area. (Colin Stone)

It is quite feasible that if the Swanage Branch had never been closed and lifted by British Rail in the early 1970s, a scene such as this would be 'the norm'. SouthWest Trains two-car No. 158881 is seen passing Creech Bottom on 20 April 2016, heading towards Corfe Castle. (Andrew P. M. Wright)

Having just passed Wyke Farm near Bradford Abbas, No. 50017 *Royal Oak* heads west towards Yeovil Junction working 1V11, the 11:00 Waterloo–Exeter St Davids, on 14 February 1991 – Valentine's Day. Due to increasing reliability problems, the Class 50s would finally be removed from the Waterloo to Exeter route in May 1992. The line would then be worked by Class 47s until the introduction of Class 159 units during 1993. (Nic Joynson)

Class 31s were always regular performers on the Yeovil to Weymouth route back in British Rail days, and Network Rail's No. 31233 continues this tradition hauling 1Q10, the 05:12 Westbury–Eastleigh via Weymouth, on 21 April 2010 past Chantmarle, a couple of miles south of Evershot Tunnel. To the rear is Class 73 No. 73107 *Spitfire*, which is the more unusual traction for this route.

An unexpected change in the weather sees the sun finally making an appearance for Deltic No. 55022 *Royal Scots Grey* as it approaches Wool with Pathfinder Tours' 'The Dorset Deltic Explorer' on 1Z76, the 15:36 Weymouth–Crewe, on 3 September 2011.

Arriva Trains Wales Class 150 No. 150270 passes Radipole on its final approach to Weymouth on 16 September 2010 in a lucky patch of sunshine.

1V72, the 17:28 Weymouth–Bristol Temple Meads summer Saturday HST service, passes milepost 151 on the 1 in 79 gradient up to the summit at Evershot, a mile away, on 17 June 2017. Led by power car No. 43191 with No. 43035 to the rear in the shadow of the trees, the train passes Chantmarle, which is home to the Grade 1 listed Chantmarle Manor, part of which dates back to 1212, although it was rebuilt in 1612. From 1951 until the spring of 1994, the manor and all associated buildings were used by the Home Office as a police training centre for Dorset Police, until it became surplus to requirements. In recent years it has been used a religious training centre and for wedding functions.

While Class 46s were regular visitors slightly further west at Weymouth, working Yeovil line services, they were not commonplace at all eastwards towards Poole, although on occasion they did appear, along with Class 45s, up until the early 1980s. The only named member of the class – No. 46026 *The Leicestershire & Derbyshire Yeomanry* – passes through Parkstone with the 'Class 46 Tribute' tour on 17 June 1984 from Weymouth back to London Liverpool Street via Portsmouth. (Colin Stone)

Slightly off the beaten track for a SouthWest Trains Class 159, No. 159016 passes Chetnole on 10 July 2013 working 5Z93, the 08:12 Basingstoke–Weymouth via Warminster and Maiden Newton. These driver route-learning trips were for Fratton drivers who were due to work the MPV (Multi-Purpose Vehicle) RHTT (Rail Head Treatment Train) circuit during the autumn leaf-fall season.

One of the star attractions at the Swanage Railway's 2014 diesel gala was privately owned Class 24 No. D5081 (TOPS number 24081), which was based at the Gloucestershire Warwickshire Railway. On 11 May 2014, No. D5081 rounds the curve at New Barn working the 13:00 Norden to Swanage service. New to traffic in 1960, this locomotive had the distinction of being the final member of a 151-strong fleet to remain in traffic. Its withdrawal came during October 1980, although it worked its final train for British Rail on 7 January 1980. With only twenty years' service with British Rail, No. 24081 has now enjoyed almost twice as long in preservation and has become one of only four of its type to be preserved.

For many years Wool has served as a rail terminal for the Army, who have had a presence in the area since 1916, when a training camp was established at nearby Bovington. These sidings were introduced in November 1918 for military rail-borne traffic, and a two-mile goods-only branch line to Bovington Camp opened a little later on 9 August 1919. The branch was short-lived and closed ten years later on 4 November 1928, although it would be 1936 before it was fully recovered. However, two of the three sidings were retained, and on 12 March 1999 No. 73136 *Kent Youth Music* and No. 73108 await departure from Wool with a loaded train formed of two VGA vans and Warwells loaded with military vehicles. (Mark Finch)

A beautiful morning over Holes Bay as a Weymouth to Waterloo service passes by on 23 November 2013.

The second Class 37-hauled test train of the day heading for Weymouth on 23 July 2012 sees Direct Rail Services No. 37603 leading its four-coach formation as it storms past Holton Heath. To the rear is classmate No. 37604, the train running as 1Q13, the 18:03 Eastleigh Works–Romsey–Southampton–Weymouth–Southampton–Lymington Pier–Southampton–Romsey–Eastleigh Works.

The LSWR Type 3A signal box at Branksome presents a handsome sight as former ScotRail Class 47/7 No. 47707 *Holyrood* passes working 2V76, the 10:20 Weymouth–Swansea, on 1 September 1990 in some superb weather.

Slightly work-stained but still cutting a fine sight is No. 33025 *Sultan* at Weymouth on 1 September 1990 before departure with 2V87, the 16:58 Weymouth–Cardiff Central. To the right stands a Class 442 Wessex Electric, and to the left stands No. 47490 *Bristol Bath Road* with 1M40, the 16:25 Weymouth–Manchester Piccadilly.

When the railway first reached Poole in June 1847, it was via a short branch line from Hamworthy Junction, off the Southampton to Dorchester railway (via Wimborne), to a terminus on the Hamworthy side of Poole Quay. Passenger services ceased on 1 July 1896 after the completion of the embankment across Holes Bay in December 1893, which connected the existing railway at Hamworthy Junction and the new line from Broadstone to Bournemouth West at Holes Bay Junction. The line would remain open for goods only and would become known as Hamworthy Goods, which is where, on 24 July 1992, Class 37/9 No. 37903 stands prior to departure with 6V99, the 13:55 Hamworthy Goods–Cardiff Tidal, formed of BDA-type wagons used to convey steel billets, which were imported by ship from Belgium. (Nic Joynson)

Coming over the junction at Branksome on 26 March 1988 is No. 33113 with a shuttle service out of Bournemouth depot in connection with the first ever open day to be held there. Some seven weeks later, on 15 May 1988, the final day of operation for Class 33/1 and 4TC units between Bournemouth and Weymouth would be seen, with the new Class 442 Wessex Electrics being introduced to Weymouth the following day.

The end to another successful diesel gala at the Swanage Railway and Nos 73213 and 73212 wait near Eldon's siding on 11 May 2010, with No. 56101, No. 73119 *Borough of Eastleigh* and BR blue 4-VEP No. 3417; the formation running as 5Z73, the 17:50 Motala Ground Frame–Eastleigh Works.

Headcode '90' in Dorset can mean only one train – the Channel Islands Boat Train. Hauled by No. 33117, and carrying the mandatory flashing light and warning bell on the front end, the train slowly makes its way along Custom House Quay in Weymouth on 6 August 1983. The train is seen running as 1W15, the 09:40 Waterloo–Weymouth Quay, connecting with the Channel Islands ferry at the quay. (John Dedman)

While running round the 05:00 Salisbury–Yeovil Junction ECS move, which was then due to form the 06:10 service to Waterloo, No. 47711 collided with coach No. 5303 at Yeovil Junction on 21 September 1991 and suffered significant front-end cab damage. After being given the go-ahead for repairs and transit, No. 47711 was hauled away on 8 October 1991 and is seen here behind classmate No. 47710 *Capital Radio's Help a London Child* while being hauled by No. 33114 with four Sealion ballast hoppers for brake force as they pass over the Yeovil to Dorchester line, and from Somerset into Dorset. (Steve McMullin)

Making a rare visit along the single-line section between Moreton and Dorchester South on 22 July 2010 is Network Rail's 'New Measurement Train' HST set, with power car No. 43014 leading, as it passes Knighton Heath running as 1Q23, the 14:51 Basingstoke–Weymouth. To the rear is power car No. 43013.

On 1 September 2012, the first day of the Paralympic sailing events at Weymouth and Portland, SouthWest Trains laid on a few additional services to Weymouth. Returning empty stock as 5Z78, the 11:56 Weymouth–Bournemouth T&RSMD, No. 159106 is seen leading No. 158881 away from Dorchester South, having worked down from Bournemouth to Weymouth earlier in the morning.

Ten years had passed since the last Voyager unit passed here. This is Wareham on 21 May 2012, and, in connection with forthcoming Olympic sailing events at Weymouth, a joint industry test run was made of the proposed timetable due to run to and from Weymouth over that Olympic period. Here, No. 221137 runs into Wareham working 1Z81, the 12:35 Bournemouth–Weymouth.

Above: A beautifully calm and still morning for the Queen and Prince Philip as they travel on the Royal Train. Having arrived overnight, and then stabled at Furzebrook on the truncated former Swanage branch, the train, hauled by an immaculately presented Class 47 No. 47539, is about to cross Rockley Viaduct on the morning of 23 March 1979, taking the royal couple to Poole for a morning of official engagements. From the *Bournemouth Evening Echo*:

> Thousands turned out for one of the most widely-enjoyed Royal visits Dorset has ever seen. But the visit started in the early hours of that Friday, March 23, when the Royal train stopped at sidings just west of Wareham. The train's arrival, at 12:59 a.m., was watched by 14 people and a dog, the Evening Echo reported the next day. A few railway enthusiasts had got wind of the visit and had waited since 10:45 p.m. in sub-zero temperatures. None of them saw the Royals, but several notebooks recorded the number of the diesel locomotive – No. 47539. The Queen and the Duke of Edinburgh arrived in Poole at 10 a.m. in gloriously sunny weather. Poole station master Jack Hurley, 65, welcomed the Queen and Prince Philip. He was set to retire the following month after 48 years on the railway.

Oposite above: It is 19 July 2002 and No. 66080 shunts the LPG terminal at Furzebrook, on the former Swanage branch. The terminal opened in December 1978 for the rail movement of crude oil extracted from the nearby Wytch Farm oil field, but by 1990 all crude was piped to Hamble oil terminal via Fawley refinery, bringing an end to this movement. However, increased production in the extraction of natural gas, which was then liquefied and moved by rail, commenced in 1990 to Hallen Marsh near Bristol, with the final train running during 2005. Long before the presence of an oil terminal at Furzebrook, clay was being transported by rail from a facility on the opposite side of the main running line when a siding was provided during 1902. Rail operations of ball clay traffic out of English China Clay's Furzebrook terminal would cease during 1992, all exports then switching to road transport. (Andrew P. M. Wright)

Oposite below: Railfreight duo Nos 20118 *Saltburn-by-the-Sea* and 20132 pass Furzebrook on 8 September 2016 with GB Railfreight's 'GBRf 15' tour from Swanage. Out of sight to the rear are GB Railfreight Class 73s No. 73213 and No. 73128, which had worked down to Swanage. Celebrating fifteen years of GB Railfreight operations, this marathon four-day tour of the country would encompass fifteen different locomotives from the GB Railfreight fleet. This was day one with the train originating from London Victoria and ending up back at Kings Cross. All proceeds from the tour went to the British Heart Foundation, The Ripple Project and Woking Homes – all charities nominated by GB Railfreight staff. (Andrew P. M. Wright)

An unidentified Class 52 Western crosses the immaculately maintained embankment at Winterborne Monkton, a mile south of Dorchester, sometime during the summer of 1974, with 1M26, the 13:00 Weymouth–Derby. Made up of ten Mk 1 coaches, the locomotive worked as far as Bristol Temple Meads. (Nigel Nicholls)

Under threatening skies, Class 442 Wessex Electric No. 2411 was spotted about to cross Holes Bay, between Poole and Hamworthy, on 2 January 2007. This was just four weeks before the Class was withdrawn from service by SouthWest Trains. (Colin Stone)

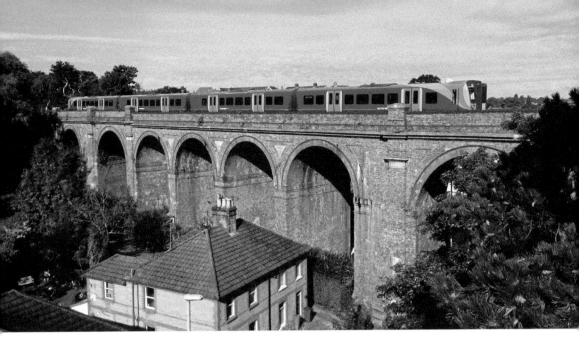

This high, seven-arch viaduct, known as Branksome Viaduct, carries the main Bournemouth to Weymouth line between Bournemouth and Branksome, and once formed part of a large triangular junction here prior to the closure of Bournemouth West station during 1965. High-capacity Desiro unit No. 450570 crosses Branksome Viaduct on 6 August 2015 while working 2B32, the 08:50 Poole–Waterloo stopping service.

Class 45 No. 45060 *Sherwood Forester* gets away from Harmans Cross and up towards Afflington Bridge, the main crossing of the A351 over the railway to Swanage, on a glorious 8 May 2009 during the annual diesel gala. Other locomotives partaking in the 2009 gala included Nos 20107, 26007, 31108, 33103, 33111 and 55022. Apart from the Class 31, which was in Railfreight grey, all other locomotives were in rail blue, creating a late 1970s vibe to the event.

Pokesdown, in the eastern suburbs of Bournemouth, and No. 47845 *County of Kent* approaches on 18 May 1994 working 1O09, the 08:18 Manchester Piccadilly–Bournemouth. Note the Second World War concrete pillbox to the right of the first coach, which still survives. The Class 47 would be re-engineered and re-numbered as Class 57 No. 57301 during 2002, and the stock would be replaced with Voyager units. (Nic Joynson)

With Class 73 No. 73107 acting as a 'translator' due to No. 56006 being air-brake only, and the coaching stock being vacuum-brake only, this unusual pairing cross Corfe Common on 9 May 2015 during the annual Swanage Railway diesel gala – the weekend event proving very popular once again.

Inside the maintenance shed at Bournemouth depot on 15 July 2008 is high-capacity Desiro unit No. 450569, as identified by the 'HC' above the unit number. Twenty-eight Class 450 units were internally modified by removing the first class seating area and replacing it with standard class 2+3 seating arrangements. Some other seating within the sets was modified, and additional hand rails were provided for high-density usage. The units were renumbered into the range 450543–450570. All modification works were carried out by Bournemouth depot; however, this seating arrangement has since been reversed and first class has been reinstated by SouthWest Trains.

To commemorate the end of loco-hauled operations on the Bournemouth to Weymouth line, a headboard was made by a couple of staff members at Bournemouth station, which read '1967 Push Pull 1987'. This is the day of unveiling, 10 October 1987, and it has been bestowed upon No. 33113 at Bournemouth. Of course, Class 33/1 and 4TC operations would continue into 1988, and the headboard would be duly corrected to read '1967 Push Pull 1988'.

Approaching journey's end, No. 47844 *Derby & Derbyshire Chamber of Commerce & Industry* is seen at the south portal of Bincombe No. 1 Tunnel, working the 10:03 Liverpool Lime Street to Weymouth summer Saturday service on 22 July 1995. Weymouth would lose its long-distance services from the end of the 2002 summer timetable when Voyager unit No. 221139 departed with the 17:15 to Manchester on 28 September 2002. All Cross-Country services thereafter started and finished at Bournemouth. (Glen Batten)

A Christmas card setting on the Swanage Railway on 18 December 2010 as its three-car Class 117 DMMU makes its way towards Harmans Cross, leaving behind the ruins of Corfe Castle, which form an imposing backdrop. (Andrew P. M. Wright)

A classic Dorset vantage point for photographers 'back in the day' as Class 442 No. 2419 is about to pass the site of Wishing Well Halt and journey into Bincombe No. 2 Tunnel with a Weymouth to Waterloo service on 30 August 1990. In the distance, Portland dominates the scene. (John Dedman)

The horse to the right doesn't appear to be too bothered as Class 46 No. 46046 shatters the peace as it storms through Upwey, working 1M26, the 13:20 Weymouth–Derby via Yeovil summer Saturday inter-regional service, during June 1977. The train was formed up of ten Mk 1 coaches on a glorious summer's day. Prior to its final withdrawal during February 1977, this service, and the corresponding inward working, 1O53, the 06:50 Derby–Weymouth, would have been a regular turn of duty for the popular Class 52 Western just a year earlier. (Nigel Nicholls)

With a friendly wave from the driver, No. 67017 *Arrow* hauls 2V67, the 16:55 Weymouth–Bristol Temple Meads, past Radipole on 24 July 2010, with a set of four retro-liveried blue and grey Mk 2 coaches.

Until the reinstatement of this working at the start of 2017 after an absence of almost five years, Class 60s were becoming increasingly rare on the stone working to Hamworthy, and in Dorset in general. One of the final workings by the class at the time, helped in no small part by their dwindling numbers, was No. 60079 *Foinaven*, which appeared on 31 March 2008. Here, the Class 60 runs round its wagons at Hamworthy Goods before returning to the Mendips, running as 7V48, the 15:00 Hamworthy–Whatley Quarry.

A glorious morning in North Dorset as former ScotRail push-pull Class 47/7 No. 47709, previously named *The Lord Provost* during its use in Scotland, approaches Sherborne on 8 September 1991 while working 1O35, the 09:28 Exeter St Davids–Waterloo. (Nic Joynson)

For a moment, this could almost be mistaken for a Gatwick Express set. However, No. 73204 *Stewarts Lane 1860–1985* is taking a Hertfordshire Railtours charter from London Victoria to Weymouth on 12 December 1992. It is seen passing Old Knowle near Winfrith, to the west of Wool. (Nic Joynson)

On the approach to Christchurch on 17 February 2015 is Cross-Country Voyager unit No. 221122 with 1O08, the 09:55 Banbury–Bournemouth. The land from here – Hawthorn Road, down to the A35 Christchurch bypass, and up to the A35 Lydhurst Road at Roeshot Hill – has been earmarked for a huge housing development, with some 875 new homes proposed by the developer.

A ten-car Class 444 Desiro unit makes its way along Christchurch Bank on 17 February 2015 in superb winter light. Sadly, overhead power lines blight the location. However, they will be buried now that the land has been approved for a large housing development to take place here.

It could almost be the 1960s as retro BR green-liveried No. 31190 approaches Sherborne on 11 November 2008 with 1Q12, the 07:59 Eastleigh Works–Exeter Riverside Yard, which was doing several trips between Salisbury and Yeovil – its two-coach test train being the perfect fit for the photographic location.

A stunning winter wonderland on 7 February 2009 as a Class 450 Desiro unit passes Winterborne Monkton, a mile south of Dorchester, on a lovely cold and crisp morning. To the centre-right the remains of a small halt still exist, which was opened on 1 June 1905 as Came Bridge Halt. It was quickly renamed to Monkton & Came Halt from 1 October 1905 until closure on 7 January 1957.

Making its way out of Poole sidings on 23 February 1992 with 'DC Tours – Solent & Wessex Wanderer 7' tour 1Z24, the 10:12 Waterloo–Weymouth–Waterloo, No. 20007 is seen leading No. 20032 and looking very out of place for the area. The Class 20s had worked the train from Eastleigh to Weymouth, having taken over from No. 56020 and No. 33116, but not before the tour had done a trip via Eastleigh depot, being hauled by No. 08847. The Class 33 had remained on the train to provide an ETH supply to the stock but was removed at Bournemouth on the way down, having developed a fault. The Class 20s continued on to Weymouth on their own. Originally, the tour engine was advertised as No. 56130, but at the last minute the loco was unavailable to work, resulting in No. 56020 substituting, and the Class 20s being provided by BR as compensation. (Colin Stone)

As part of a visit by the Queen and the Duke of Edinburgh on 11 June 2009 to Weymouth, and other parts of Dorset, the royal couple travelled by train, which was hauled by No. 67006 *Royal Sovereign*. Once the royal party had alighted at Weymouth, the Royal Train quickly departed empty coaching stock back to Wolverton, this time being worked by No. 67005 *Queen's Messenger*. As would be expected, both locomotives and the coaching stock were immaculately presented as they emerged from the north portal of Bincombe Tunnel near Winterborne Monkton.

General Manager's Saloon No. TDB975025, hauled by departmental grey Class 33/1 No.33109, arrives at Maiden Newton on 8 October 1992, forming 2Z01, the 08:05 Clapham Junction–Clapham Junction via Salisbury, Templecombe, Yeovil Junction, Yeovil Pen Mill, Weymouth, Bournemouth and Southampton. (Steve McMullin)

With public sector workers on strike, including fire fighters, Steam Dreams' 'Cathedrals Express' tour on 10 July 2014 was diesel-hauled, replacing the planned steam traction, to reduce fire risks. West Coast Railways Class 37 No. 37706 approaches Worgret Junction with the return working: 1Z87, the 17:06 Swanage–Victoria.

An incredibly rare working on the morning of 28 November 1998 finds Class 55 Deltic No. 55022/D9000 *Royal Scots Grey* at the head of 1M01, the 06:36 Poole–Liverpool Lime Street service, which is seen here at Poole prior to departure. Tucked inside is Class 47/7 No. 47703. (Colin Stone)

No. 444007 sweeps round past Redbridge, near Moreton, working a Weymouth to Waterloo service on 22 June 2010 on a fine summer's evening.

Heading out of Poole for Weymouth is Class 442 No. 2412, working the 06:40 service from London Waterloo on 30 August 2000. In the sidings is the HST set for the 09:05 Poole to York, formed of power cars No. 43086, closest to the camera, and No. 43160 at the far end, which will lead the train. (Colin Stone)

A Western Region mechanical Class 101 DMMU approaches Upwey on 8 September 1987 while working 2O54, the 09:05 Westbury–Weymouth.

Wessex Electrics Nos 2404 and 2408 pass Pokesdown on 9 September 1995, working the 09:48 Weymouth to Waterloo service. (Nic Joynson)

Driving straight into preservation on 21 March 2009 is SouthWest Trains Class 121 'bubble-car' No. 960012 *John Cameron*, which is seen here at Quarr Farm crossing, near Harmans Cross, while running from Bournemouth depot to a new life on the Swanage Railway.

A fine winter's morning as petroleum sector No. 60028 *John Flamsteed* approaches Wareham on 28 January 1994 with an LPG working from Eastleigh to Furzebrook. (Nic Joynson)

UK Railtours' 'The Juniper Factor' Class 458 farewell tour on 23 May 2015 approaches Poole with No. 8006 leading No. 8014 and running as 1Z45, the 09:02 Waterloo to Poole, which is running fifteen minutes late.

Running alongside the River Frome on 18 January 2017 at East Stoke, to the east of Wool, is No. 444018, working 1W12, the 10:03 Weymouth–Waterloo. The River Frome rises at Evershot and flows down to Poole Harbour, a distance of some 35 miles, running through Maiden Newton, Dorchester and Wareham. Frome is an old Celtic river name meaning 'fair' or 'fine'.

Hertfordshire Railtours' 'Inter-City Merrymaker – Weymouth Awayday' stands at Weymouth with No. 31128 *Charydbis* leading classmate No. 31452 *Minotaur* on 26 August 2007, both in matching Fragonset livery, and with InterCity-liveried No. 31454 *The Heart of Wessex* on the rear. The train was running as 1Z31, the 18:18 Weymouth–Minehead.

Direct Rail Services (DRS) Nos 20311 and 37610 make their way through Poole while heading for Winfrith, to the west of Wool, with a nuclear flask working on 9 August 1999. DRS had recently taken over the contract for the working of all flask trains from EWS in the February of 1999. (Mark Finch)

Seen on 10 August 2011 is former Gatwick Express Class 460 No. 460004 on Bournemouth depot, minus the distinctive sloping 'nose cone', prior to conversion to a five-car Class 458/5. Works to convert these distinctive eight-car units would be undertaken at Wabtec Doncaster, and Brush of Loughborough, with all eight units in the class being treated – the first two sets entering service during March 2014 after a period of testing. SouthWest Trains now use the 'new' Class 458/5 units on suburban services out of Waterloo. (Steve Clark)

Since re-connection with the national network, Swanage has become a popular destination for railtour promoters and 24 September 2016 was no exception as the GB Railfreight Class 73 pairing of No. 73109 and No. 73107 *Tracy [Will You Marry Me?]* approach Wareham with UK Railtours' 'The Purbeck Adventurer' as 1Z63, the 07:45 Tonbridge–Swanage.

The unique silver livery of EWS Class 67 No. 67029 *Royal Diamond* certainly stands out on a fine day as it awaits departure from Swanage on 16 June 2010 with UK Railtours' 'Purbeck Tornado' to Waterloo. (Andrew P. M. Wright)

The first of two Class 37-hauled test trains to Weymouth on 23 July 2012 sees Network Rail's No. 97304 (previously No. 37217) *John Tilley* sweep round towards Stratton – between Maiden Newton and Dorchester West – hauling 3Z14, the 09:43 Bristol–Weymouth–Swindon–Bristol, on its outward run down to Weymouth on a fine summer's day. This is the only known visit to Dorset by this departmental variation of the Class 37 on a test train.

A fine summer's evening at Christchurch as 4-CIG No. 1740 arrives on 11 July 1994 working a Victoria to Poole service, as indicated by the '46' on the headcode blinds. (Nic Joynson)

2016 proved to be another fantastic year for the Swanage Railway when its annual diesel gala attracted a record number of visitors. Although the gala is now in its tenth year, this would be the first Class 40 to attend, the honour falling to No. D213 *Andania* courtesy of the Class 40 Preservation Society, seen here on 8 May 2016 working the 13:00 Swanage to Norden service.

Another one of the star attractions at the 2016 Swanage Railway diesel gala, Class 46 No. D182 (TOPS number 46045) in its striking 'chromatic blue' livery heads the 13:20 Norden to Swanage service on 8 May 2016.

Passing the Up distant for Maiden Newton, petroleum sector-liveried Class 47 No. 47197 accelerates southwards with 2O87, the 08:03 Cardiff Central–Weymouth, on 4 September 1991. During the summer of 1991, this service, and the corresponding return working – 2V87, the 16:58 Weymouth–Cardiff Central – was diagrammed for a petroleum-sectored Class 47, the booked locomotive for the summer being No. 47381. However, other members of the class operated the service on several occasions, bringing some welcome variety. (Steve McMullin)

Owing to electrical supply problems between Dorchester and Weymouth, SouthWest Trains was unable to run their regular electric service on 19 June 2015. Hastily drafted in from Salisbury, and off its normal Waterloo to Salisbury/ Exeter route, No. 159108 operated an hourly shuttle service from Dorchester to Weymouth. Seen here, on what would be one of its final trips before a normal service was restored after repairs were under taken by Network Rail, the Class 159 is seen near Bincombe Tunnel running as 2W86, the 17:03 Weymouth–Dorchester South.

Carrying the unofficial painted name *Victory* along the top-centre of the engine compartment, above the BR double arrow, No. 09025 is stabled for the weekend at Bournemouth depot on 8 August 1987. Running down to Hamworthy Goods on a Monday morning, it would be out-based there until its return on Friday afternoon. Periodically, the '350' would be swapped, generally on a Sunday night, with another shunter from Eastleigh, as Bournemouth depot lost its allocation of shunting locomotives in the 1970s. By 1992 the requirement for a Class 08/09 at Hamworthy Goods would finish, bringing to an end their use in Dorset.

A glorious afternoon in the county of Dorset as Colas Railfreight Class 67s, led by No. 67027, pass through Dorchester West on 10 May 2017, working 1Z22, the 08:14 Tyseley LMD–Bristol High Level Sidings via Weymouth. To the rear is No. 67023. Both locomotives were acquired from DB Cargo by Colas Railfreight towards the end of 2016, specifically for use on high-speed test trains. After overhaul and repaint, they were released to traffic during March 2017.

SouthWest Trains Class 458/5 No. 458534 is seen stabled on Bournemouth depot on 7 October 2013 under a threatening sky. These five-car units were a rebuild of the Class 460 units formerly used on the Gatwick Express and were intended for use on suburban services out of Waterloo. To the left stand depot shunters Nos 73235 and 73133, which were restricted to use within the confines of the depot only. (Steve Clark)

Having arrived with 1O09, the 08:17 Manchester–Bournemouth train, locomotive No. 47784 *Condover Hall* has now run round the stock and awaits departure with the back working, 1M14, the 14:20 Bournemouth–Manchester, on 20 June 1998. The services were booked for a HST but a last-minute loco-hauled substitution brought a very rare visitor to the consist – West Coast DVT No. 82129, as seen behind the Class 47.

Running round their stock at Bournemouth on 27 June 1998 is Dutch-liveried Class 31 No. 31466 and Regional Railways variant No. 31465, which had arrived on 1O38, the 09:10 Edinburgh–Bournemouth. The pair returned north on 1M81, the 18:14 to Manchester. This service was notorious during the summer of 1998 for producing unusual traction due to a shortage of serviceable Virgin Cross-Country Class 47s. It was also a day of unusual locomotives through Bournemouth as just in front of this working were No. 58039 and No. 58047, which had worked up from Weymouth with the Worksop Open Day Committee's Worksop Wessex Wanderer back to Worksop.

On the approach to Bournemouth is blue-grey DMMU set No. B434 with set No. B460, which was in promotional British Telecom livery of all-over yellow, working the 12:55 Weymouth–Bristol Temple Meads on 24 May 1986. The yellow-liveried DMMU was nicknamed *Buzby* after a small yellow bird used in BT television adverts and other advertising platforms.

Three-car DEMU No. 207017 departs Sherborne on 4 April 1993, working the 09:25 Yeovil Junction to Salisbury service. From an original fleet of nineteen units that were principally intended for use in south-east England, three were to survive into preservation after the final units had been withdrawn from the national network during 2004. This unit was one of those three and would find a new home at the Spa Valley Railway. (Nic Joynson)

Great evening light in the county of Dorset on 14 June 2017 as Class 158 No. 158798 passes Burl Farm at Hollywell working 2O94, the 14:50 Great Malvern–Weymouth. The unit is in a unique and distinctive pale blue finish, with the advertising stating that it is 'supporting North Somerset children with additional needs', which highlights a children's charity and the work they do. Just beyond the rear of the train is the site of the former station of Evershot (although the village of Evershot itself is just over a mile away), which closed on 3 October 1966. The former double-track main line has stiff climbs from both directions to the summit, which is a few yards beyond the tin shed in the distance, and in the days of steam would almost certainly have required banking assistance. In the Down direction from Yeovil, the line constantly rises to this summit with the final climb being at 1 in 51 to Evershot Tunnel, and in the Up direction from Maiden Newton the line again constantly rises, with the section where the Class 158 is seen being at 1 in 69.

Nothing unusual about the traction but the only occasion of a Great Western green-liveried Class 47 working a Virgin Cross-Country service train into Dorset was No. 47846 *Thor*, seen here in the sidings at Poole prior to working Sunday's 1S97, the 15:05 Poole to Glasgow Central, on 16 August 1998. This locomotive was re-engineered as a Class 57 and was renumbered as No. 57308. It is currently in use with Direct Rail Services.

Again nothing unusual about the traction as such because Class 47s were after all common in Dorset. What makes this slightly more interesting is that under the privatised railway, freight locomotives were becoming increasingly rarer to find on Class 1 passenger services – even more so when it involved air-conditioned stock that required electricity provided by a passenger variant Class 47. However, No. 47095 found itself on the business end of 1O10, the 09:13 Liverpool–Weymouth, on 29 August 1998. Here, the Railfreight Distribution-liveried Class 47 is seen at Weymouth having run round its stock before heading to Bournemouth depot empty stock.

No mistaking where this is. Yet again, the Swanage Railway welcomes another new visitor, this time in the form of a First Great Western HST set, seen here led by No. 43028 on 28 September 2013 while running into Corfe Castle. Promoted as 'The Cotswold Purbeck Express', the train ran as 1Z12, the 07:32 Worcester Shrub Hill–Swanage, although it would only get as far as Corfe Castle due to concerns about gauging issues. However, a second HST set, this time operated by East Midlands Trains, ran though from Sheffield to Swanage on 14 June 2014. (Andrew P. M. Wright)

From the end of steam in 1967 through to the introduction of electric services to Weymouth in 1988, the Class 33/1 and 4TC formations worked up and down between Bournemouth and Weymouth. One such service is seen here at Redbridge, near Moreton, as No. 33116 propels 4TC No. 8024 on the 14:32 from Weymouth on 22 September 1987. Note the newly laid conductor rail as part of the upgrade works. (Nic Joynson)

The line from Weymouth to Westbury via Yeovil is about as close as you will get to the lamented Somerset & Dorset route that ran from Bath to Bournemouth. Passing through the beautiful Dorset countryside near Evershot Tunnel is a First Great Western Class 150 unit with a service from Weymouth on 22 May 2010.

It is hard to imagine that this was once a double-track main line. No. 67027 *Rising Star* heads along the single line towards Evershot on 28 August 2010 while hauling four ex-Anglia liveried coaches, working 2V67, the 16:55 Weymouth–Bristol Temple Meads summer Saturday service.

With its seven-coach formation, No. 37427 *Bont Y Bermo* approaches Thornford with the 16:53 Weymouth–Cardiff Central on 22 August 1989. Note the telegraph poles and cables behind the locomotive and coaches – a once common feature alongside the railways around the country. (Nic Joynson)

Two Class 444 Desiro units pass over Holes Bay on 1 February 2017 under quite stormy-looking conditions – their white livery certainly stands out in the gloom. Holes Bay was dissected by the construction of the railway embankment, which opened in 1893 and directly links Hamworthy and Poole. Two structures were provided: Creekmoor Viaduct at the Poole end and Upton Viaduct at the Hamworthy end. The two trains have just passed over Creekmoor Viaduct.

History in the making on 1 April 2009 as the first passenger charter runs on to the Swanage Railway. DB Schenker Class 66 No. 66152 crosses from Network Rail and onto Swanage Railway at Motala Ground Frame, between Furzebrook Sidings and Norden, under the watchful eye of Network Rail's operations staff. This was 'The Purbeck Pioneer' tour running as 1Z98, the 08:45 Victoria–Swanage. Such was the popularity of the charter that a repeat run ran the following day, utilising the same stock and locomotive and running in the same pathways. (Andrew P. M. Wright)

On its first visit to Dorset in the new Aggregates Industry livery, No. 59001 *Yeoman Endeavour* – with 'bell end' leading – prepares to get away from Hamworthy Goods on 17 September 2008 back to Whatley Quarry with the stone empties.

New Class 442 Wessex Electric No. 2401 exits Bournemouth depot on 12 February 1988 and comes across the junction into Branksome with a test run to Brockenhurst some three months before the full introduction of these units on the Waterloo to Weymouth line.

Regarded as one of the finest EMUs to operate on Britain's railways, the BREL Derby-built fleet of twenty-four Class 442 Wessex Electric units certainly exude a stylish appearance, both externally and internally, and were unlike anything seen on the Southern Region at the time. On 12 February 1988, No. 2401 is seen passing the 1886-built LSWR Type 3A signal box at Branksome while working a test train from Bournemouth depot to Brockenhurst.

A change of stock for the recently introduced trial public service between Swanage and Wareham on 30 June 2017. West Coast Railways Class 37 No. 37516 *Loch Laidon* arrives at Corfe Castle with the London Transport 4TC set, fresh out of Eastleigh Works following an extensive restoration and finished in London Transport red livery. The train ran as No. 5Z38, the 14:35 Eastleigh Works–Swanage. The Class 37 would then return the four loco-hauled coaches that had been working the service for the last two weeks back to the West Coast Railways depot at Southall. (Andrew P. M. Wright)

In some stunning autumnal light, BR blue electro-diesel No. 73201 *Broadlands* passes through the Dorset heathland near Winfrith on 18 October 2011 working 1Q08, the 05:27 Eastleigh Works–Eastleigh Works via Fareham, Eastleigh, Weymouth, Portsmouth and Southampton. To the rear, Network Rail yellow classmate No. 73138 tails this four-coach test train.

West Coast Railways No. 47500 hurries past Holton Lee, between Holton Heath and Hamworthy, on 29 November 2010 with No. 5Z97, the 12:45 Motala Ground Frame–Southall empty coaching stock move. To the rear is steam locomotive Class 5 No. 44932. The locomotives and stock had worked 'The Bath & Bristol Christmas Express' from Poole on 25 November 2010, with the train then being stabled at Swanage for the weekend upon its return to Poole due to engineering work between Brockenhurst and Millbrook. The train finally headed back to base on the Monday.

A Winfrith to Gloucester move conveying a nuclear flask sandwiched between two barrier wagons and a guard's brake van, and hauled by Class 73 No. 73134 *Woking Homes 1885 – 1985*, gets away from Dorchester South on 25 August 1992. The sidings at Winfrith, two miles west of Wool, are on the 'Down side' of the railway line heading towards Weymouth. Therefore, all trains out of the sidings are required to run to Dorchester South to allow the locomotive to run round its train before heading back up and onwards to its final destination. (Nic Joynson)

A lightweight load for heavyweight Class 37 No. 37884 on 17 May 1989 as it passes Branksome working 6V99, the 14:52 Hamworthy Goods–Cardiff Tidal Sidings. New to traffic on 7 November 1963 as No. D6883, under the creation of TOPS it would be re-numbered as 37183, and for a time during the 1980s it carried the name *Gartcosh* while in traffic in Scotland. Re-numbered to 37884 from 1 January 1988, the locomotive is still in use during 2017 under the ownership of Europhoenix and sporting their stylish livery. It is often hired out for use by other operators such as Rail Operations Group or Colas Railfreight.

The final locomotive-hauled service train out of Weymouth on 4 September 2010 was hauled specially by green-liveried Class 57 No. 57604 *Pendennis Castle* and was strengthened to five coaches to cope with expected demand from enthusiasts. Usually a booked Class 67 diagram, the train approaches Thornford running as 2V67, the 16:55 Weymouth–Bristol Temple Meads, in a lucky patch of milky sunlight.

Large-logo No. 73207 passes Poole Park's Victorian boating lake on 31 July 2014 hauling 1Q05, the 06:15 Eastleigh Works–Eastleigh Works via Hamworthy Goods and Weymouth. Although just out of sight, BR blue-liveried No. 73201 *Broadlands* trails to the rear of the four-coach test train.

No. 159103 blows up a storm in its wake near Motcombe, to the east of Gillingham, on 18 January 2013 as it leads a six-car train from Waterloo to Exeter. (Mark Pike)

On 22 July 1995, No. 47837 passes through Christchurch working 1E43, the 09:00 Poole–York. Note some of the steam-age fixtures still present in the mid-1990s, such as the former unloading dock with concrete loading gauge and the white wooden gate leading to it. To the left of the locomotive a cast concrete milepost (painted yellow), and of course the relatively unchanged station dating back to 1886 can also be seen. (Nic Joynson)

Not your everyday traction type in Dorset as Class 20 No. 20901 *Nancy* leads a Bristol to Weymouth weed spray train past Stratton, between Maiden Newton and Dorchester West, with No. 20904 *Janis* at the rear on 10 April 1992. (Nic Joynson)

A DRS pairing of No. 37605 and No. 37609 pass from Somerset into Dorset as they depart from Yeovil Junction and on up towards Sherborne on 19 April 2007. The leading locomotive and first coach are in Dorset and the trailing locomotive and three rear coaches are in Somerset – the county boundary being the fence post above the cab of No. 37605 and going across the railway beyond the tree to the left. (Mark Pike)

Proudly wearing the Union Flag, but disrespectfully covered in graffiti along the bodyside, No. 66707 *Golden Jubilee* heads past East Stoke and alongside the River Frome on the eastern approach to Wool on 11 April 2015 with No. 6G16, the 12:52 Eastleigh yard–Dorchester South engineer's train, in connection with track renewals between Bincombe Tunnel and Upwey.

It is the Swanage Railway's 2017 diesel gala and, courtesy of the Peak Locomotive Company, No. 45041 *Royal Tank Regiment* crosses Corfe Common with the 09:15 Norden to Swanage service on the first full day of the three-day event on 5 May 2017.

One of the highlights of the Swanage Railway's 2017 diesel gala was the use of a Colas Railfreight Class 56 to celebrate the company's tenth anniversary of rail operations in the UK. On 5 May 2017, No. 56096 leads one of the Swanage Railway's resident Class 33s, No. 33111, past Afflington Bridge and down towards Harmans Cross. Colas had originally planned to send Class 47 No. 47749 *City of Truro* in addition to the Class 56; however, due to main line commitments, Colas were unable to release it for the weekend. (Steve Clark)

Transrail-liveried No. 37505 and EWS-liveried No. 37174 stand at Hamworthy Goods during 1998, having run round the stone empties after unloading up near Hamworthy station. The train will then return to the Mendips running as 6V89, the 17:50 Hamworthy–Merehead. (Mark Finch)

Across Creech Heath on 6 October 2015 comes No. 66848 with a train load of auto-hoppers of spent ballast, which are destined for the south-end of Furzebrook as part of embankment stabilisation works. The embankment here suffered from erosion over the years and would form part of the upgrade works between Worgret Junction and Norden prior to the introduction of a trial public daily service between Swanage and Wareham by the Swanage Railway. (Andrew P. M. Wright)

In the twilight of Class 50 usage on the west of England route, No. 50030 *Repulse* approaches Sherborne on 7 September 1991 with the 15:15 Waterloo–Exeter St Davids service. By 24 May 1992 the Class had worked their final services between Waterloo and Exeter, which would then be taken over by Class 47s. (Nic Joynson)

With two Class 33/1 failures at Weymouth on the Bournemouth to Weymouth line services, a quick substitution by two Class 47s was required to maintain the service. Quickly pressed into service to cover the failures were No. 47115 and No. 47639 *Industry Year 1986*. Sporting a silver roof that is generally associated with Stratford depot, No. 47115 awaits departure from Weymouth on 11 June 1986 with No. 1W42, the 17:35 to Waterloo formed of 4TC set No. 414.

1998 proved to be a very poor year for Class 47 availability on Virgin Cross-Country – so much so that various other classes of locomotives would be substituted by those in control to cover for these shortfalls. One such train that became near legendary for turning out unusual traction was Saturday's No. 1O38, the 09:10 Edinburgh–Bournemouth, and 1M81, the 18:14 Bournemouth–Manchester Piccadilly back working. Possibly one of the rarest locomotives to work this train was Class 56 No. 56019 on 20 June 1998, seen here at Bournemouth prior to departure with the return working to Manchester.

On the approach to the eastern portal of the 742-yard-long Buckhorn Weston Tunnel, or Gillingham Tunnel, at Bugley, is No. 47708, which is working an additional 09:05 Paddington–Paignton on 9 June 1991. Upon arrival at Templecombe the locomotive would be officially named *Templecombe*, and the temporary covering over the nameplate on the bodyside would be removed. The returning special would run back to Paddington via Taunton and the Berks & Hants route. (Nic Joynson)

Once upon a time, Weymouth saw a procession of additional trains to and from the seaside town via the Southern and Western routes that converge at Dorchester. On 28 September 2002, Weymouth had seen its last long-distance service when Virgin Cross-Country Voyager No. 221139 *Lief Eriksen* departed with the 17:15 to Manchester. Thereafter, all Cross-Country services terminated at Bournemouth. First Great Western, however, still provided strengthened trains on the Western route on summer weekends and a HST set is seen on 21 June 2014 between the tunnels at Bincombe with 1V67, the 17:28 Weymouth–Bristol Temple Meads, with power car No. 43092 leading. To the rear, No. 43144 is just inside Bincombe No. 2 Tunnel.

A throwback to the 1960s and 1970s when the 'Hymek' diesel-hydraulic locomotives were regular visitors to Dorset, operating to Weymouth and Poole. With headcode '1M09' recreating the 16:29 Poole to Birmingham service of 1971, which would have been hauled by a Hymek, No. D7076 crosses Corfe Common heading for Norden on the evening of 9 May 2015 during the Swanage Railway's annual diesel gala.

The view from Hog Cliff Bottom on a cold but glorious start to the morning sees No. 37407 *Blackpool Tower* get away from Maiden Newton on 19 April 1995, working the 06:40 Westbury–Weymouth service. In the distance, to the left, can be seen Rampisham Down transmitting station, which totalled twenty-six transmitter pylons and was one of the main transmitters of the BBC World Service until closure, the final broadcast being on 29 October 2011. Demolition of the decommissioned pylons commenced on 9 January 2013. (Nic Joynson)

Loco-hauled trains on the Waterloo to Exeter line had recently finished in favour of Class 159 units but No. 33116 was despatched on 31 August 1993 with six coaches from Eastleigh to collect coach No. 17073 from Honiton. Having been detached from a service train with a brake defect and dumped in the siding for six months, this was clearly an invitation too great for the vandals to resist and the coach is covered in graffiti. As the train passes Bradford Abbas running as 5Z19, the 12:19 Honiton–Eastleigh T&RSMD, the additional coaches provide brake force. (Steve McMullin)

With ownership of the line being transferred from Network Rail to the Swanage Railway from the original boundary – known as Motala Ground Frame, at 129 miles, 55 chains – to a new maintenance boundary just south of Worgret Junction, at 126 miles, 51 chains, the ground frame and associated trap points plus gate were recovered. Passing the site of Motala Ground Frame is the first passenger train to run up to the new Swanage Railway/Network Rail boundary, south of Worgret Junction, using this two-car DMMU on 25 July 2016. (Andrew P. M. Wright)

Class 27 No. D5401 (TOPS numbers 27056 and 27112) from the Northampton Type 2 Group was one of the stars at the 2012 Swanage Railway diesel gala. Here it is seen heading for Swanage on 12 May 2012 in superb condition – the veteran diesel looking and sounding fantastic.

Working 3Z14, the 09:20 Bristol East–Bristol East via Weymouth and Swindon, on 17 November 2011, BR blue Class 31 No. 31106 gets away from Maiden Newton a few minutes late, heading towards Dorchester during a lucky break in the cloud.

About to pass from Dorset into Somerset on 31 August 2014 is No. 150246, leading No. 150238 past Clifton Maybank, near Yeovil, working 2V86, the 16:10 Weymouth–Bristol Temple Meads. Telegraph Hill, near Minterne Magna, dominates the background.

A couple of weeks into the newly reinstated stone train from the Mendips, after an absence of almost five years, Westbury's 'super shunter' Class 60 No. 60054 makes its third visit on 17 February 2017 as it arrives at Hamworthy Goods with the empties after unloading near Hamworthy station. The locomotive will run round its train before heading back to Whatley Quarry.

Looking and sounding absolutely superb, No. D1015 *Western Champion* sweeps round the curve towards Stratton, between Maiden Newton and Dorchester West, on 7 September 2013 while hauling 'The Western Wessexman' – 1Z52, 05:53 Leicester–Weymouth. These locomotives were no stranger to this former Western Region double-track main line as they regularly worked down to Weymouth from Westbury and Bristol.

Colas Railfreight Class 70 No. 70809 departs Furzebrook on 16 April 2015 with empty spoil wagons and heads back towards the possession limit board at Worgret Junction, before gaining access back onto the Waterloo to Weymouth main line. The train ran as 6C18, the 19:08 Worgret Junction–Eastleigh East Yard. The train was dropping spent ballast just south of Furzebrook to help build up an embankment that had been eroded over the years by vegetation encroachment and deer crossing the railway. (Andrew P. M. Wright)

Against the setting sun on 22 June 2014, Nos 159006 and 159020 pass Lenthay Crossing, on the approach to Sherborne, working 1L76, the 19:25 Exeter St Davids–Waterloo.

West Coast Railways Class 33 No. 33029 *Glen Loy* rounds the curve towards Worgret Junction while hauling the Swanage Railway-organised 'Purbeck Explorer II' tour on 11 May 2014, running as 1Z33, the 17:15 Swanage–Ealing Broadway. With the London Underground 4TC in tow, this was the first Class 33 and 4TC working from Swanage to Wareham since October 1969.

Sporting the rather distinctive, and stylish, Europhoenix livery, No. 37611 *Pegasus* leads its four-coach test train over Mead Farm crossing – about three quarters of a mile south of Yetminster station – on 14 June 2017, working 1Z22, the 08:14 Tyseley LMD–Bristol High Level Siding via Weymouth. To the rear is classmate No. 37608 *Andromeda*.

Against the low winter sun, SouthWest Trains Class 444 Desiro unit No. 444023 heads westwards over Holes Bay towards Hamworthy working 1W69, the 14:05 Waterloo–Weymouth service, on 18 January 2017.

Ten years after being deemed non-standard by SouthWest Trains (SWT), who withdrew the class in early 2007, the Class 442 Wessex Electric is making a return with new franchise operator First/MTR – under the branding of South Western Railway – who took over the SWT routes from Stagecoach on 20 August 2017. Prior to their re-introduction, principally on the Portsmouth to Waterloo route, the units require overhaul, repainting and branding, and have been progressively moved from storage at Ely to Bournemouth depot by Rail Operations Group. On 14 September 2017, Class 47 No. 47812 hauls Nos 2418 and 2414 through Poole, running as 5O86, the 09:06 Ely Papworth Sidings–Bournemouth depot. A total of eighteen units from a fleet of twenty-four will be used by the new Train Operating Company.

Death of a Salesman

Arthur Miller

Oxford
Literature
Companions

Notes and activities: Su Fielder
Series consultant: Peter Buckroyd

OXFORD

UNIVERSITY PRESS

Contents

Language | 58

Themes | 74

Performance | 84

Critical Views | 94

Skills and Practice | 102

Glossary | 118

What are Oxford Literature Companions?

Oxford Literature Companions is a series designed to provide you with comprehensive support for popular set texts. You can use the Companion alongside your play, using relevant sections during your studies or using the book as a whole for revision.

Each Companion includes detailed guidance and practical activities on:

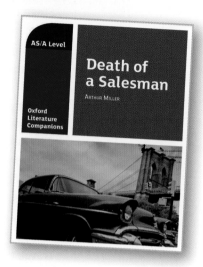

- **Plot and Structure**
- **Context**
- **Genre**
- **Characterization and Roles**
- **Language**
- **Themes**
- **Performance**
- **Critical Views**
- **Skills and Practice**

How does this book help with exam preparation?

As well as providing guidance on key areas of the play, throughout this book you will also find 'Upgrade' features. These are tips to help with your exam preparation and performance.

In addition, in the extensive **Skills and Practice** chapter, the 'Exam skills' section provides detailed guidance on areas such as how to prepare for the exam, understanding the question, planning your response and hints for what to do (or not do) in the exam.

In the **Skills and Practice** chapter there is also a bank of **Sample questions** and **Sample answers**. The **Sample answers** are marked and include annotations and a summative comment.

How does this book help with terminology?

Throughout the book, key terms are highlighted in the text and explained on the same page. There is also a detailed **Glossary** at the end of the book that explains, in the context of the play, all the relevant literary terms highlighted in this book.

Which edition of the play has this book used?

Quotations and character names have been taken from the Penguin Modern Classics edition of *Death of a Salesman* (ISBN 978-0-14-118274-2).

How does this book work?

Each book in the Oxford Literature Companions series follows the same approach and includes the following features:

- **Key quotations** from the play
- **Key terms** explained on the page and linked to a complete glossary at the end of the book
- **Activity boxes** to help improve your understanding of the text
- **Upgrade** tips to help prepare you for your assessment

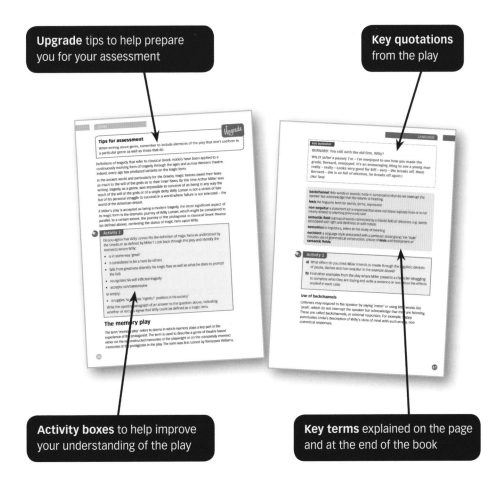

Upgrade tips to help prepare you for your assessment

Key quotations from the play

Activity boxes to help improve your understanding of the play

Key terms explained on the page and at the end of the book

Plot and Structure

Death of a Salesman is a play in two acts followed by a brief scene, described by the playwright as a **Requiem**.

In each Act, as Willy interacts with the other characters, he suffers intermittent 'hallucinations' about things that have happened to him in the past. He also receives several 'visitations' from his dead brother Ben. None of the other characters is aware of what is distracting Willy during these episodes, which are introduced by brief musical **refrains**.

> **refrain** in music, a repeated melody or tune
>
> **requiem** a religious service, piece of music or poem designed to honour the dead

Plot

For the purposes of this summary, the Acts have been divided into smaller episodes.

Act One

Episode 1

The play opens with Willy Loman, the salesman of the title, arriving home late at night from a sales trip to Portland that he has had to abandon. He explains to his wife Linda that he started **'dreamin''** while he was driving and that he feared causing an accident. Linda is relieved to have him home safely and tries to relax him and persuade him to go to bed, but he is very agitated. She urges Willy to try to persuade his boss Howard to find him a selling job in New York, where they live, so that he doesn't have to exhaust himself travelling so much. Encouraged by this prospect, Willy becomes calmer.

Linda tells Willy that their two grown-up boys Biff and Happy have been out for the evening and we learn that Biff, the elder brother, has just come home from Texas and that the younger Happy has moved back home for a while, so that they can enjoy time together.

Willy complains that he can't fathom the fact that Biff, **'a young man with such – personal attractiveness'** is so **'lost'** and moving from one low-paid, manual job to another.

Episode 2

The focus of the action shifts to the boys' bedroom, where Biff and Happy are discussing their adolescence, the girls they have had and their present lives. Biff reveals that he is never happier than when he is working outdoors, while Hap complains about waiting for promotion in the store where he works. Both seem dissatisfied and both talk about wanting to get married. As they talk about the future, they can hear Willy talking loudly to himself downstairs.

Activity 1

In pairs, discuss the boys' attitudes towards the girls they have 'had'. What does this reveal to you about the place of women in the society that Miller is depicting?

Consider how their views are juxtaposed with the conventional representation of wifeliness that Miller has shown us in Linda's tender concerns for Willy.

Episode 3

The focus shifts to the kitchen where Willy is completely absorbed by re-living an episode from the past. He talks aloud to the unseen Biff and Hap as if they are teenagers again. Then the actors who play the characters of Biff and Hap as adults appear on stage and assume their teenage roles. Willy praises Biff for his skill in polishing his car. In Willy's memory, the two boys idolize their father and he tells them that one day he will own his business and **'I'll never have to leave home any more'**. The boys respond enthusiastically to the idea of joining Willy on one of his trips up to New England. Willy revels in Biff's footballing prowess and his promise to dedicate a **'touchdown'** to Willy in the next game.

In Willy's memory, his two sons idolize him and he is very proud of Biff's footballing prowess; Royal Shakespeare Company, 2015

Still in the memory, Bernard, Biff's nerdish neighbour from school, arrives to try to get Biff to study with him for his maths exam, but neither Biff nor Willy take any notice of him. Willy dismisses Bernard as **'a pest'** and **'an anaemic'**, and foresees that his boys will outstrip Bernard in the end because Willy claims that **'in the business world, the man who creates personal interest, is the man who gets ahead'**.

A younger-looking Linda enters into Willy's fevered memory and he recalls her totting up his weekly earnings and trying to balance the housekeeping money. Willy exaggerates the profits he has made from his sales but Linda manages not to dent his pride as she tells him how much money they owe, down to the last cent.

Still in the past, Linda attempts to console Willy when he has a crisis of confidence about people laughing at him. Linda declares Willy to be **'the handsomest man in the world'**, but then a disturbing sound effect of a woman's laughter is heard and this gets louder as a further, more troubling memory pushes Linda out of Willy's head and he is transported to a hotel bedroom in Boston where the Woman he has just slept with is preparing to leave.

Willy's thoughts become more turbulent as the *'the Woman disappears into the dark'* and he is overcome by recollections of Biff's youthful, reckless behaviour, as voiced by Linda and Bernard – stealing a football, being too rough with girls, driving the car without a licence, and not working hard enough for his maths exam. These painful memories cause him to cry out and the real Happy to come down, in his pyjamas, to try to find out what is troubling his father.

Activity 2

Identify moments in the text where transitions between past and present (real-time) action occur. How might the difference between past and present action be made clear to an audience of the play? You might consider staging, use of props, the vocal and/or physical skills of the actors, use of sound and/or lighting.

Episode 4

Hap's real-life presence brings Willy out of his disturbing recollections briefly, but he is still agitated. Willy remonstrates with himself about missing out on the opportunity that his brother Ben offered him, many years before, to join him in Alaska and make his fortune. We see that Willy values financial success above all other satisfactions in life.

Willy reacts dismissively to Hap's promise to support his father in his old age, **'I'm gonna retire you for life'**, raising his voice in desperation as he recognizes his predicament as a travelling salesman who **'can't drive a car!'**

The commotion has roused Willy's neighbour Charley, who arrives in his dressing-gown and slippers to see if he can help. Seemingly used to Willy's odd behaviour, Charley sends Hap back to bed and plays cards with Willy to try to settle him down. He offers Willy a job, which Willy refuses.

As they play cards, Willy's dead brother Ben materializes, and Willy and he converse about the past. Only hearing Willy's side of the conversation (since Ben's comments are in Willy's head), Charley is bewildered by Willy's apparently random replies to Ben's questions. Willy accuses Charley of not playing their game of cards properly and Charley leaves the house. Willy continues to talk to his dead bother about how Ben made his fortune in diamond mines.

Willy slips back into his imagined past, introducing Ben to Linda and his boys, and listening to Ben's tales of his financial successes. Willy boasts to Ben about the **'fearless'** nature of his sons and we hear that Willy is encouraging them to steal building materials from the construction company next door. Ben offers nothing but approval of the way Willy is raising his sons, calling them **'Outstanding, manly chaps'**, reassuring Willy that he is right to teach them to value material wealth.

> **Key quotation**
>
> **Can't you stay a few days? You're just what I need, Ben, because I – I have a fine position here, but I – well, Dad left when I was such a baby and I never had a chance to talk to him and I still feel – kind of temporary about myself.**
> *(Willy)*

> **Activity 3**
>
> Look back through Act One so far. What evidence can you find that Miller wants his audience to think about the kind of role model that Willy is for Biff and Happy?
>
> Write a series of bullet points that you could use in an answer to a question about fathers and sons in the play.

Ben walks out of the scene repeating his catchphrase, **'by God, I was rich'**.

Episode 5

In real time, Linda comes downstairs to see where Willy is and finds that he has gone outside. Biff and Happy both come down, complaining about Willy's erratic behaviour. Linda chastizes them both for abandoning Willy. She tells them that his firm has stopped his salary, that he is on 'commission only' and not selling anything anymore. She explains that Charley is giving him $50 a week, which Willy claims to Linda is his pay.

> **Key quotation**
>
> **He's not the finest character that ever lived. But he's a human being, and a terrible thing is happening to him. So attention must be paid. He's not to be allowed to fall into his grave like an old dog.**
> *(Linda)*

Linda also reveals that some of Willy's recent accidents in the car have been failed suicide attempts and that he has prepared and hidden a short piece of rubber tubing to attach to the gas pipe in the cellar in order to kill himself. This moment of revelation encourages the audience, as well as Willy's sons, to adjust their perception of the man who previously appeared to be simply old and tired.

All of this is shocking news to the boys. Linda tries to find out from Biff what happened to sour the relationship that he used to have with his father, but Biff only reminds her that it was Willy who threw him **'out of this house'**, claiming that it was because he found out that Willy is **'a fake and he doesn't like anybody around who knows'**. Nevertheless, Biff promises to stay in New York and get a job.

Episode 6

Willy comes in from the yard and seems to have emerged from his hallucinations. He is initially quite aggressive with Biff, whom he feels has been insulting him. When Hap comes up with the idea of he and Biff going into business together, selling sporting goods under the brand name of Loman Brothers, Willy's mood is transformed to one of boundless optimism.

Biff's original vague notion that he might seek a loan from Bill Oliver, a previous employer, is seized upon by Willy who sees an opportunity for Biff to become the kind of success that he had always dreamed of for him. Willy gives Biff a stream of advice about how to secure Oliver's backing, which includes lying about the work he has been doing.

> **Key quotation**
>
> Tell him you were in the business in the West. Not farm work.
> *(Willy)*

The family go to bed more optimistic than they have felt for a very long time. Linda sings to Willy to soothe him to sleep. He does not answer her question about what Biff might have against him.

As Willy expresses his determination to talk to his boss about a job in the New York office, in the cellar Biff discovers the rubber pipe that Willy has prepared to take his own life. The curtain falls as Biff removes the pipe from its hiding place and climbs the stairs to his bedroom.

Act Two

Episode 7

Act Two begins with Willy at the breakfast table, drinking coffee and feeling refreshed. As Linda tells him about Biff starting out early to see Bill Oliver, Willy feels confident of a positive outcome. He tells Linda that one day they are 'gonna get a little place out in the country' and grow vegetables and keep chickens. He fantasizes about the boys coming to stay with their families, emphasizing Miller's interest in the American Dream and its location in the succeeding generations.

Linda reminds Willy to ask his boss for 'a little advance' as well as for a job in the New York office, as they have outstanding bills to pay, including their final payment on the 25-year mortgage on their house.

She delights Willy by telling him that the boys want to take him out that night and treat him to an evening meal. Willy is thrilled by the idea and leaves with a light heart. As soon as Willy leaves, Linda gets a phone call from Biff. She is bursting to tell him that Willy seems to have changed his mind about the rubber tube, so is disappointed to hear that it was Biff who removed it from its hiding place. She begs Biff to be kind to his father.

> **Key quotation**
>
> And be sweet to him tonight, dear. Be loving to him. Because he's only a little boat looking for a harbour.
> *(Linda)*

Episode 8

The scene shifts to the office of Howard Wagner, Willy's boss and the son of the man who first employed Willy, over 30 years before. Willy's request to give up travelling and move to working permanently in New York is met with a flat refusal and a reminder that, as the play persistently demonstrates, **'business is business'**.

Willy is angry. He pleads with Howard to find him some work and tells him he only needs $50 a week. Howards tells him he no longer wants Willy either in New York or as a travelling salesman. In despair, Willy ends up yelling at his boss, who is adamant that he must pull himself together before instructing him to **'stop by and drop off the samples'**. Willy's employment of over 30 years comes to a brutal end.

> **Key quotation**
>
> I put thirty-four years into this firm, Howard, and now I can't pay my insurance! You can't eat the orange and throw the peel away – a man is not a piece of fruit!
> *(Willy)*

Episode 9

When Howard leaves Willy in his office to calm down, Willy, exhausted and highly distressed, imagines his brother Ben. Ben doesn't have much time but he offers Willy a role to **'look after things'** for him in Alaska. Willy is tempted by the idea, **'Me and my boys in those grand outdoors'**, before the younger Linda enters the delusion and talks Willy out of the idea. Linda is scornful of Ben's obsession with chasing a fortune.

> **Key quotation**
>
> LINDA [*frightened of Ben and angry at him*]: Don't say those things to him! Enough to be happy right here, right now. [*To Willy, while Ben laughs*] Why must everybody conquer the world? You're well liked, and the boys love you, and someday – [*to Ben*] – why, old man Wagner told him just the other day that if he keeps it up he'll be a member of the firm, didn't he, Willy?

Cheered by Linda's confidence in him, Willy revels in the likely future success of Biff, but Ben turns away, reminding Willy of the opportunities to be had in **'a new continent'** and concluding, as ever, with the tantalizing prospect of becoming **'rich'**. Willy is defiant, however, calling after the vision, **'We'll do it here, Ben'**, showing his unwillingness to take on the role of adventurer and absentee father or to abandon his family.

> ### Activity 4
>
> Do you think that Linda has held Willy back by being so satisfied with their life? Or is this memory a distortion of events and a way of Willy blaming someone else for his own lack of adventure? Write a paragraph about each possibility.

Willy's pride in the young Biff leads him into another vivid encounter with the past and he relives the day of Biff's greatest triumph on the football pitch as the captain of the All-Scholastic Championship Team of the City of New York. Willy remembers his feelings of pride in his son, as Hap and Bernard compete for the privilege of carrying Biff's helmet into the clubhouse.

Willy also remembers Charley's jokey tone as he pretends not to understand the significance of the game. Willy is incensed by Charley's refusal to be impressed, to the extent that he is ready to fight his neighbour, **'Put up your hands'**.

Willy is so proud of Biff's triumph on the football pitch that he cannot understand that Charley values other talents more highly; from the 1951 film, starring Fredric March as Willy

Episode 10

The memory fades and the scene shifts to the present as Willy finds himself in the reception area of Charley's office. He meets Bernard, who has made a success of himself as a lawyer. When Bernard enquires about Biff, Willy blusters and lies to him about his success, telling him that Bill Oliver had **'Called him in from the West'** where Biff has been **'doing very big things'**.

Willy suddenly asks Bernard why Biff didn't **'ever catch on'**, a tacit admission that Biff is not successful. Bernard seems reluctant to discuss Biff with Willy. Finally, he identifies Biff's trip to Boston, when he went to talk to his father about flunking maths, as the turning point in Biff's whole attitude about his future. Bernard tells

Willy that after the trip to Boston, Biff had **'given up his life'**. Willy feels that he is being blamed for Biff's failure and he becomes angry. Bernard leaves to **'argue a case in front of the Supreme Court'**, which is a tremendous achievement for the boy who Willy and Biff used to mock for his studiousness.

Charley offers Willy a job, one of many such offers he has made him, but Willy refuses, even though he admits that he has been fired by Howard.

> **Key quotation**
>
> I – I just can't work for you, Charley.
> *(Willy)*

Although not prepared to work for Charley, Willy is prepared to borrow money from him and, on this occasion, he asks for $110 dollars to pay for his insurance. Charley is angry with Willy but out of compassion lends him what he needs. Willy concludes that he is **'worth more dead than alive'**, an idea that Charley is quick to quash, insisting, **'Willy, nobody's worth nothin' dead'**. In a rare moment of tenderness, Willy tells him, **'Charley, you're the only friend I got.'**

Activity 5

Do you think Willy deserves Charley's friendship? Look back over the play so far and make a list of any examples where Willy appears to be a friend to Charley or worthy of his friendship and where Willy is shown not to be Charley's friend.

Episode 11

The scene moves to the restaurant where Biff and Happy are supposed to be treating Willy to a big meal. Hap is the first to arrive and he starts flirting with a young woman, offering her champagne. When Biff arrives, Hap introduces him as a great football player and tries to impress her. Forgetting the purpose of the meal, Hap persuades the girl to find a friend so that he and Biff can have a double date.

Biff is highly agitated, having waited to see Bill Oliver all day only to discover that he did not remember Biff at all. Biff has stolen Oliver's fountain pen, in a moment of madness, before running down eleven flights of stairs, arriving at the restaurant in a state of despair and determined to tell Willy the truth.

> **Key quotation**
>
> Hap, he's got to understand that I'm not the man somebody lends that kind of money to.
> *(Biff)*

Hap encourages Biff to keep Willy happy by telling him that Oliver is thinking about the proposition. Willy arrives and immediately wants to know how Biff got on. As Biff tries to tell Willy the truth, Hap keeps cutting him off and trying to put a positive spin on everything.

Willy's troubled brain struggles to keep the hallucinations at bay. First he imagines Bernard telling Linda that Biff had **'flunked math'**. Then, tormented by his guilt, Willy becomes unstable, hearing the laughter of the Woman and striking Biff who he calls a **'rotten little louse'**.

The girl that Hap was flirting with returns with a friend for Biff, while Biff is showing a confused Willy to the washroom. Biff confronts Hap with the rubber tubing that Willy had hidden and accuses Hap of not giving **'a good goddam about him'** before leaving the restaurant. Hap and the girls follow him out.

Activity 6

What point do you think Miller is intending to make through Hap's prioritizing of the chance of sexual conquest above the well-being of his father?

Episode 12

Willy is now alone in the washroom and his hallucination engulfs him. He is back in Boston, in bed with the Woman, when Biff knocks on the hotel bedroom door to tell his father about flunking maths and to persuade him to return to New York with him to talk to his teacher. When he discovers that Willy has a woman in his room, Biff is devastated. He calls Willy a **'phony little fake'** before leaving his father grovelling on the floor.

As Willy shouts at Biff, **'come back here or I'll beat you'**, Stanley the waiter at the restaurant enters the washroom and breaks the news to Willy that his sons have left with the girls. Dazed, Willy asks if Stanley knows where he can buy seeds.

Episode 13

The scene changes back to the Loman house. Happy and Biff are returning from their night out. Happy has a bunch of roses for his mother, which she knocks out of his hand. Linda speaks harshly to Biff and Hap, disgusted by their abandonment of Willy after having offered to take him to dinner. She calls the girls that Hap and Biff went out with **'lousy rotten whores'** and orders her sons out of the house.

Biff is chastened but Happy pretends that he has done nothing wrong, insisting that Willy **'had a swell time with us'**. Biff goes outside to see Willy, who is planting seeds in the dark, using a flashlight to guide him.

While Biff and Linda look on, Willy's fevered brain sees Ben moving towards him and he asks for Ben's advice about killing himself, to gain the $20,000 life insurance payout. Once Ben has confirmed, **'twenty thousand – that *is* something one can feel with the hand, it is there'**, Willy seems more cheerful. He anticipates Biff's shock when, at Willy's funeral, Biff will see how popular his father was. He looks back on the good times before Biff became disillusioned with him.

When Biff tries to tell Willy that he is leaving and not coming back, Willy accuses him of doing everything to spite him. He won't shake hands with Biff and yet he doesn't want him to leave. This precipitates a moment of crisis in the play.

Biff maintains that 'We never told the truth for ten minutes in this house!' He confesses to having been in jail for three months in Kansas for stealing a suit and he blames Willy for filling him so full of 'hot air' so that he couldn't take orders from anybody. A bitter row breaks out between father and son before Biff breaks down.

Key quotation

Pop, I'm nothing! I'm nothing, Pop. Can't you understand that? There's no spite in it any more. I'm just what I am, that's all.
(Biff)

Sobbing into his father's arms, Biff awakens in Willy the sense that he is loved by the son he has always adored. He decides to kill himself so that Biff can use the insurance money to 'be magnificent'.

The phantom brother Ben approves of Willy's decision, describing it in the language of business as 'A perfect proposition all around', thus sealing Willy's fate. Ignoring the pleas of Linda to come to bed, Willy rushes out. The sound of the car starting and moving away brings Linda and the boys hurtling downstairs to try to prevent the inevitable.

The curtain falls on a **tableau** of Linda, in mourning clothes, supported by Charley and accompanied by Biff, Hap and Bernard as the funeral party move to the front of the stage where Willy's grave is imagined to be.

> **tableau** a brief scene when the actors are seen quite still, without moving, on stage

Requiem

After the funeral, attended only by Linda, Biff and Happy, Charley and Bernard, Linda asks sadly, 'Why didn't anybody come?' She struggles to understand this and also why Willy killed himself just as they had paid off their mortgage. Biff says that Willy 'had the wrong dreams', but Hap fiercely disagrees, vowing to stay in the city and carry on pursuing Willy's dream 'to come out number-one man'.

Linda has a moment alone to say goodbye to her husband. She apologizes for not being able to cry but does begin to sob as she asks him, 'Why did you do it?' just now when they are free of the worry of the mortgage. The final lines of the play, 'We're free', are a poignant and ironic end to the play.

Writing about plot

In your assessment you may have the opportunity to discuss the significance of certain aspects of the plot but you will never be asked simply to recount the story of *Death of a Salesman*.

You may be asked to consider Miller's dramatic methods in presenting the plot in the fractured way that he does, using memories, hallucinations and conversations with the dead to illuminate Willy's thought processes.

Track through each episode of memory and hallucination, considering how they reveal Willy's thoughts and fears.

Structure

Structuring of events

Every work of literature is shaped by its writer into recognizable structures. Novelists use chapters, poets use stanzas or verses, and playwrights conventionally use acts and scenes to divide drama into shorter segments.

The **external structure** of *Death of a Salesman* comprises two acts and a requiem. The two acts depict the final 24 hours in Willy Loman's life, while the requiem takes place on the day of Willy's funeral. By structuring the main action to unfold over a 24-hour period, Miller employs a device often referred to as 'unity of time', compressing the action and intensifying the audience experience of events as they develop.

The **internal structure** of the play is far from linear since the present-day timeline is interspersed and mingled with memories and imagined events. This **non-linear structure** flickering between past and present, presents Willy Loman's fractured perceptions of reality for the audience.

> **external structure** the physical shape of a piece of literature, determined by the way its content is arranged and presented by the writer
>
> **internal structure** the sequencing of events in a piece of literature, whether chronologically or otherwise
>
> **non-linear structure** a plot that does not proceed chronologically

Unity of time

This is one of the three unities that were devised by the 17th-century French dramatist Jean Mairet, based upon the writings of the Greek dramatic critic Aristotle in his book *Poetics*. While Aristotle identifies only unity of action as a prerequisite of tragedy, Mairet and other neo-classicists in France and Italy enshrined three unities into their definition of tragedy:

- unity of action (one main plot with few diversions or subplots)

- unity of time (the action should be take place over no more than 24 hours)

- unity of place (the action should take place in a single location representing a single place).

However far Miller intended to emulate the structure of Greek or neo-classical models of tragedy, it is clear that the play's action is unified in its coherence around Willy Loman's fate and family, that it takes place in a 24-hour period and that the majority of the action takes place either in the Lomans' family home or in Willy's head.

Another major influence upon Miller's structuring of the play can be seen in the plays of Henrik Ibsen. In particular, Miller appears to have embraced Ibsen's characteristic retrospective structure whereby a crisis arises in the present as a result of the gradual revelation of a crucial event from the past. Linda highlights the significance to Willy of Biff's return in Act One:

> **Key quotation**
>
> **When you write you're coming, he's all smiles, and talks about the future, and – he's just wonderful. And then the closer you seem to come, the more shaky he gets, and then, by the time you get here, he's arguing, and he seems angry at you. I think it's just that maybe he can't bring himself to – to open up to you. Why are you so hateful to each other? Why is that?**
> *(Linda, Act One)*

We can see, then, how Biff's return, which occurs only shortly before the play begins, is critical in sparking Willy's memories of his son's 'golden' potential. It also becomes clear, as the play develops, that Biff's return is also responsible for prodding Willy's guilty conscience about his betrayal of Linda, which results in his psychological collapse.

Miller's approach to time, as a structural device, differs from previous tragic models in that Willy's experience of time is unique. Rather than simply showing Willy's past impinging on his present actions over a 24-hour period, Miller presents the past and the present co-existing for Willy to such an extent that it is not always clear to him, or to the audience, which is which.

Realism and expressionism as structural influences

Miller originally intended to give the play the title of 'The Inside of His Head' to indicate that much of the dialogue in the play occurs within Willy's mind and reflects his mental state and perception of reality. Although Miller abandoned that title, the play's subtitle of 'Certain Private Conversations in Two Acts and a Requiem' also gives the flavour of this internal dialogue.

Nevertheless, Miller employs many structural features of **realism**, locating much of the action in the realistic present and anchoring the development of the story within external time. Realistic family relationships are presented and the dialogue between the husband and wife, the brothers and the neighbour Charley is written in a colloquial, realistic style.

Each act is arranged in a similar way with a series of sequences that take place in the dramatic and realistic present but, as the plot unfolds, the realistic action is punctuated with an almost equal number of sequences that take place in Willy's head and which depend upon a co-existent **expressionistic** structure.

Some of the expressionistic sequences appear to be Willy's re-lived memories, especially from when Biff and Happy were in their teens. Others, involving the Woman principally, could be memories or could be imagined episodes from the past. The third type of expressionistic sequence involves the visitations of Willy's dead brother Ben. Miller uses the expressionistic structural device of introducing varied musical refrains to announce the shifts from the present to the past or from the real present to a present that includes an exchange between Willy and Ben. Ben does not always feature as a figure from the past; some of his appearances occur

Many important sequences take place in Willy's head, played here by Antony Sher in the Royal Shakespeare Company's 2015 production

and have an impact on the unfolding plot in the present. Sequences that are not part of the objective present but take place in Willy's idealized past with his family are also heralded by musical refrains or lighting effects that create the impression of the disappearance of the apartment blocks surrounding the Loman home and the appearance of leaves covering the building.

expressionism a form of theatre that originated in Germany in the early 20th century in which characters' inner feelings and/or thoughts are expressed outwardly in a form of physical expression or represented through concrete staging elements such as setting, lighting and/or sound

realism a genre of literature that attempts to create a faithful representation of life

Activity 7

Read the extract from **'Well, I think he was going to...'** to **'Boy, you must really be makin' a hit.'** *(Act One)* and think about how Miller moves between the realistic and expressionistic sequences.

In the extract above from Act One, no two intersections are quite the same. Miller juxtaposes the real-time conversation of the brothers with Willy's experience of the past in a different part of the house. Elsewhere, past and present moments collide, involving characters who exist in real time conversing with Willy, who is inhabiting two separate time zones simultaneously.

Not that all the sequences set in the past are memories. In Act Two (from **'Tell me what happened!'** to **'You took Oliver's pen?'**) Willy re-lives an episode that he can only ever have experienced second-hand, begging the question of whether he is just as creative in the sequences that he did actually experience for himself.

Activity 8

Complete a version of the table below, which shows where each of the 'scenes' (1 to 9) take place: in real time, in Willy's memory, or in his imagination. You may find that some scenes have elements of memory and imagination. Think about why and find a way to record this.

Note what triggers Willy's shift from real time on each occasion. Think about why.

Act One	Real time	Memory	Imagination	Trigger
1	Willy returns. Willy and Linda talk.			
2	Biff and Happy discuss their adolescence, their lives, jobs and futures.			
3		Willy warns Biff about girls and talks to the boys about starting his own business. Bernard arrives and Willy mocks him. Linda appears; she and Willy discuss his earnings and their debts.		Willy's memory about Biff polishing his Chevvy, as he talks to Linda, sparks this memory.

Reality and imagination

The two acts are similar in the way that reality and imagination alternate. They are completely opposite, however, in terms of the development of the mood of the drama.

Act One begins pessimistically with Willy's sombre realization that he cannot continue as a travelling salesman. It ends on a note of great optimism with all the family looking forward to Biff and Hap's commercial success as Loman Brothers.

Act Two begins optimistically. Willy is refreshed and determined to land a job in New York and Biff has made an early start, intent on securing funding for the new venture. It ends tragically as Willy sacrifices himself for the sake of financial reward for his son.

Use of conventional dramatic structures

Despite the play's unconventional division into real and imagined episodes, the major events in the play's action are presented within a conventional dramatic structure common to almost all drama and consisting of five stages: **exposition**, development, **complication or reversal**, **climax**, and **denouement**.

> **climax** the highest or most intense part of the play
>
> **complication or reversal** conflicts or problems that threaten or reverse the protagonist's progress
>
> **denouement** the resolution of the plot
>
> **exposition** introduction of key information about setting, characters and situation to help the audience make sense of the play

Exposition

The opening sequence of the play offers the audience a very clear exposition of the salient features of Willy's situation:

- Willy is in his 60s; he is a travelling salesman and **'tired to the death'** *(Act One)*; he is anxious about his elder son.
- Willy's wife Linda is caring and supportive.
- His elder son Biff is 34 and a drifter from job to job; he loves the outdoors and scorns office work and sales.
- There is friction between Willy and Biff; at one time, Willy threw Biff out of the house.
- Willy's younger son Hap works in a store but is unfulfilled.
- All of Willy's family is concerned about his deteriorating mental state.

Development

The development of the real-time narrative takes place over the two acts:

Act One

- Willy begins to exhibit signs of mental disturbance or extreme fatigue.
- Willy's delusions and habit of talking to himself disturb his sons, who confront Linda about his state of mind.
- Linda confides in her sons that Willy's car 'accidents' were attempted suicides and that she found some rubber tubing Willy prepared to fix to the gas tap.
- Biff promises his mother that he will stay in New York and **'make good'** *(Act One)*.
- Biff and Happy persuade Willy and Linda that they are going to raise money and go into business together as Loman Brothers, selling sports equipment; the family is united and elated.

Act Two

- Linda tells Willy that she is about to make the last payment on the mortgage on the house and that the boys have invited Willy to dinner.
- Willy goes to see his boss Howard to ask if he can have a job in the New York office.

Complication or reversal

The complications/reversals occur in Act Two:

- Howard refuses to give Willy a job at the New York office; he fires him instead.
- Biff tells Happy about his futile attempt to see Bill Oliver, his theft of the fountain pen and his realization that his whole life has been a **'ridiculous lie'** *(Act Two)*.
- What should have been a celebratory dinner turns into a fiasco as Willy refuses to listen to Biff's facts.
- While Willy retires to the men's room, overcome by his memories, Happy and Biff leave him alone and escape with the two girls Happy has picked up.

Climax

There are a few key moments leading up to the climax where Willy realizes that Biff has always loved him:

- Linda chastises her sons for abandoning their father at the restaurant.
- Biff insists on talking to Willy despite Linda's protest; his attempt to shake hands with Willy is rebuffed.
- The intense exchange between Biff and Willy leads to Biff confronting his father with the rubber tubing.
- Biff's confession to being **'nothing'** culminates in his emotional breakdown as he clings onto his father and sobs *(Act Two)*.
- Willy's recognition and surge of self-worth.
- Willy exits hastily and there is the sound of a crash.

Denouement

The denouement occurs in the Requiem.

- Nobody comes to Willy's funeral apart from his immediate family, Charley and Bernard; his dream of a **'massive'** funeral *(Act Two)* is not realized.

- Biff concludes that his father had **'the wrong dreams'** and also that he **'never knew who he was'** *(Requiem)*; Biff comes to understand his own nature.

- Charley delivers the verdict that **'Nobody dast blame this man'** *(Requiem)*.

- Hap swears to continue Willy's quest to be **'number-one man'** *(Requiem)*.

- Linda says her farewell to Willy and confesses not to understand why he has killed himself; her assertion of freedom as the curtain falls, has a hollow ring.

Activity 9

The descriptions above of the five stages of the drama relate to the chronological plot and what happens to Willy and his family in real time. Create a chart that shows how Willy's interactions with his brother Ben relate to these stages.

Although Miller follows dramatic conventions in structuring the events of the play, it is also important to recognize some of his departures from convention. The most significant of these is the positioning of the revelation scene set in the Boston hotel room where Biff discovers his father's adulterous behaviour and condemns him as

In his memory, Willy realizes that Biff's discovery of the Woman in the hotel room is the moment when the father–son relationship starts to deteriorate; from the 1951 film, starring Fredric March as Willy

a 'fake' (Act One). This revelation does not act as a turning point to the action (as it would in a more conventionally structured drama) since it is a memory of a past event already known to Willy and Biff, and never disclosed to Linda or Happy, who remain ignorant of Willy's betrayal of Linda to the end. Its function is to reveal to the audience why Biff and Willy have a 'hateful' relationship (Act One) and to prepare us for their final reconciliation.

This revelatory sequence, acted out in Willy's memory, is effectively summoned by Willy's chance encounter with Bernard, who asks him point blank, 'What happened in Boston, Willy?' (Act Two). Bernard's question provokes an angry reaction from Willy, who immediately tries to deflect the blame for Biff's perceived failure in life from himself: 'What are you trying to do, blame it on me? If a boy lays down is that my fault?' (Act Two). His defensive reaction indicates that Willy is in denial about his own contribution to Biff's aimless existence.

Importantly, however, Miller builds in a structural delay between the trigger of the memory (Bernard's question) and the re-enactment of Biff's discovery of the Woman in Willy's room. In between these two moments, Willy has a rational conversation with Charley about Bernard's achievements and about parenting, and he arrives at the Chop House for dinner, anxious to hear how Biff has fared with Bill Oliver. This delay, and the temporary drop in dramatic tension that it occasions, actually helps to intensify the impact of Biff's discovery of the Woman. This supplies the audience with the missing piece of the jigsaw for the cause of the discordant father–son relationship and heightens the pathos of Willy's total collapse in the men's room.

Writing about structure

Make sure that you know and understand the specialist vocabulary associated with the conventions of drama:

- unities of action, place and time
- realism and expressionism
- exposition, development, complication/reversal, climax, and denouement.

By using specialist terminology correctly and authoritatively in your assessment, you will be able to express yourself more concisely and effectively.

You may well be asked to comment on the play's dramatic structure, on the ordering of events and on the dramatic effects Miller creates by placing one particular sequence of action next to another. For example, consider the effect created in Act One by placing Willy's declaration of devotion to Linda, 'You're the best there is, Linda, you're a pal, you know that?' immediately before the first scene with the Woman, who tells Willy, 'I think you're a wonderful man'.

Biography of Arthur Miller

- Arthur Miller was born in New York City on 17 October 1915 into a prosperous family of Jewish émigrés. His father was a successful manufacturer of ladies' coats.

- In 1929, after the economic disasters of the Wall Street Crash and the Great Depression, Miller's father's business was ruined and the family had to move to a smaller house in Brooklyn.

- Arthur was not a well-motivated student, preferring sporting endeavour over academic study, and he graduated from high school with unimpressive grades.

- He had to work in a car parts warehouse to earn the money to attend the University of Michigan, where he enrolled on a journalism course. It was at Michigan that he wrote his first plays. They earned him numerous student awards, so he switched to an English degree and took courses in play-writing, graduating in 1938.

Arthur Miller (1915–2005), with the director Elia Kazan (left), on the Broadway set of *Death of a Salesman* in 1949

- Miller returned to New York and began a career writing for radio.

- He married his college sweetheart Mary Slattery in 1940 and they had two children.

- Miller's first successful play was *All My Sons* (1947). Directed by Elia Kazan, it was a 'well-made' play, influenced by Miller's study of Ibsen.

- *Death of a Salesman*, also directed by Kazan, followed in 1949 and ran for a year and a half. It was an outstanding success, winning six Tony Awards, including Best Play and Best Author for Miller. Miller was also awarded the 1949 Pulitzer Prize for Drama. The play has been in production in America, and world-wide, ever since, including a production directed by Miller himself and performed in Chinese at the Beijing People's Art Theatre in 1982.

- *The Crucible* (1953), Miller's play about the witch trials in Salem, Massachusetts, was his next big success, followed by *A View from the Bridge* in 1955.

- Miller divorced his first wife and married Hollywood star, Marilyn Monroe in 1956, but the marriage did not last and they were divorced in 1961. Marilyn committed suicide shortly afterwards.

- In 1957, Miller appeared before the House Committee on Un-American activities to explain his association with Communist groups. Although Miller gave details about his own membership of groups sympathetic to communism, he was convicted of 'contempt of court' for refusing to give the names of others who attended such groups.

- In 1962, he married his third wife Inge Morath, an Austrian-born photographer.
- Miller's play, *After the Fall*, generally considered to be based on the disintegration of his marriage to Marilyn Monroe, was produced in 1964.
- His later plays, including *Incident at Vichy* (1964), *The Price* (1968) and *Broken Glass* (1993), did not receive the acclaim of the plays he wrote in the 1940s and 50s but did nothing to tarnish his reputation as one of the greatest playwrights of the 20th century.
- Arthur Miller died in February 2005 at the age of 89.

Historical context

The Great Depression

When Miller wrote *Death of a Salesman* in 1949, it was only a few years since the end of the Second World War in 1945. The exact year of the play's setting is not specified, but it is assumed to be set around the same time as it was written, sometime just after the end of the war.

The time period covered by the action of the play represents the final 24 hours of Willy Loman's life, but the historical context, both of that 24 hours and of the memories that press in upon Willy, is significant.

The fictional Willy Loman, in his early 60s when the play is set, has lived through and survived the Great Depression in America, which started with the Wall Street Crash in 1929. The 'Crash' refers to the collapse of the American stock market, which resulted in the whole country being plunged into a catastrophic, economic downturn, pushing many banks, corporations and small businesses into insolvency and causing individual families to lose everything they had owned.

The only date that is mentioned in the play is 1928, the year before the crash. Willy tells Howard that **'in 1928 I had a big year. I averaged a hundred and seventy dollars a week in commission'** (*Act Two*). Although this claim is disputed by Howard, Miller is hinting that 1928 would have been the most successful year of Willy's fictional career before the Great Depression blighted the economy.

During the Great Depression, which lasted for almost ten years, finances were tight for most American families, including Miller's own. There was mass unemployment and ordinary people struggled to put food on the table. All non-essential spending was reined in.

A significant fact to bear in mind is that when the Great Depression began, the United States was the only industrialized country in the world without some form of unemployment insurance or social security. In 1935, Congress passed the Social Security Act, which for the first time provided Americans with some form of unemployment and disability benefits and modest pensions for old age. There was no such relief for the unemployed before 1935, making Willy's dread for the future very real.

> **Key quotation**
>
> ... when business is bad and there's nobody to talk to. I get the feeling
> that I'll never sell anything again, that I won't make a living for you, or a
> business, a business for the boys.
> *(Willy, Act One)*

As in any major financial recession, manufacturers, and the salesmen who represented them, struggled to sell goods in a diminished market. Many salesmen, along with office workers and even government workers were simply made redundant. Families had to resort to borrowing money to buy household necessities. Like the Loman family, they would make regular instalment payments for items such as refrigerators, washing machines and vacuum cleaners, often spread over several years.

Miller has provided a context for the Loman family in which financial security is a daily concern. Willy's dream of **'Someday'** having his **'own business'** (*Act One*) appears even more unrealistic in the setting of the early 1930s, when he shares his thoughts with the teenage Biff and Happy.

Nevertheless, 17 years or so later, it appears that Willy and Linda have survived the recession, against the odds. We learn that Linda and Willy have had a mortgage for 25 years, which they took out when Biff was nine, and that they are about to make the final payment on it. Considering Willy's earlier fears about making a living, the final payment on their mortgage is a real achievement. Unfortunately, Willy undervalues this **'accomplishment'** (*Act Two*), as Linda rightly describes it, comparing himself unfavourably with his more successful neighbour Charley and with his wealthy, entrepreneurial brother, Ben.

It was the coming of the Second World War that eventually saved America's economy and, in the immediate post-war years, the financial climate changed. The economy, which had struggled to survive during the 1930s, improved dramatically. Manufacturing industry was given a huge boost by the need to produce modern weaponry, aircraft and ships for the war effort. By the time the war ended in 1945, manufacturers turned their attention to harnessing the technological advances that had helped to win the war to create advances in domestic machinery.

The late 1940s saw a huge increase in car ownership and in household goods such as washing machines, refrigerators, vacuum cleaners, record players and tape recorders. The acquisition of a good standard of living with luxury goods and cars, available to all who worked hard enough, became part of what has become known as the American Dream.

> **Activity 1**
>
> Why do you think Miller created two distinct economic contexts for the play? Write a paragraph about the importance of the intersecting time periods in the play.

The American Dream

The familiar term of 'the American Dream' was first coined by historian James Truslow Adams in his 1931 book *The Epic of America*. However, he did not invent the concept. The notion of the American Dream is based upon America's Declaration of Independence (1776), which stipulates that 'all men are created equal' with the right to 'life, liberty and the pursuit of happiness'. This ideal was envisaged long before the advent of heavy industry in America, long before the railways, and long before success was measured in sales made or deals brokered.

In the nineteenth century, when Willy's father was making a living selling flutes, **'right across the country'** (*Act One*), the American Dream for many US citizens was focused on acquiring and cultivating their own land. Raising crops, sheep or cattle was seen as a highly desirable occupation. Thomas Jefferson, who was the president at the start of the 19th century, believed that for the nation to be successful it depended upon an independent, virtuous citizenry and he particularly advocated the ownership of small farms. Jefferson's maxim that 'Those who labour in the earth are the chosen people of God' sat comfortably with an appreciation of the 'great outdoors' as well as an appreciation of the value of manual labour.

> **Thomas Jefferson**
>
> Jefferson (1743–1826) was the main author of the Declaration of Independence and the third US president, so he was a leading figure in America's early development.

America was considered to be a land of opportunity, where the pioneering spirit was admired and emulated. Willy's long lost father represents this spirit of enterprise. Willy's father seems to be the source of Willy's love of the 'great outdoors' and although he seems to have abandoned his family when Willy was only three, he may also be the source of Willy's choice of career – travelling great distances in the hope of making a good living through sales.

Activity 2

Look at what Ben says about his and Willy's father:

Father was a very great and a very wild-hearted man. We would start in Boston, and he'd toss the whole family into the wagon, and then he'd drive the team right across the country; through Ohio, and Indiana, Michigan, Illinois, and all the Western states.

(Ben, Act One)

Do you see anything 'great' or enviable in his lifestyle and his treatment of his family? Write two paragraphs about his achievements and the likely effect of his choices on Willy's outlook on life.

By the early decades of the 20th century, the American Dream extended the democratic ideals of the American Constitution to include the opportunity for all well-motivated and hard-working citizens to achieve prosperity and success. Specifically, it enshrined the ideal of upward mobility, or the idea that living standards and social improvement would improve, from generation to generation. For James Truslow, in 1931, the attainment of the American Dream was less to do with the acquisition of money and material goods, such as cars and luxuries, and more to do with each individual attaining the fullest stature they were capable of and of being recognized and valued for what and who they were.

The spectre of the American Dream haunts Willy Loman as he looks back on what he sees as his meagre accomplishments in comparison to those of his brother and his neighbour. However, it is easy to see how the idea of the Dream relating to being recognized and valued as an individual informs Linda's insistence that Willy should have **'attention'** paid to him as a **'person'** irrespective of the fact that he is neither 'a great man' nor **'the finest character that ever lived'** (*Act One*).

It is also easy to see how Willy Loman's sense of entitlement to be prosperous and to have successful sons has been fuelled by the American Dream. Willy's sense of his own personal failure as a father and a breadwinner, combined with Biff's spectacular lack of progress in materialistic terms, impel Willy towards suicide. Miller does not condone the American Dream; he exposes it for the corrosive force it can become.

Travelling salesmen

When Miller wrote *Death of a Salesman* at the end of the 1940s, the career of the travelling salesman was well established in the country and can be seen to play a significant part in bolstering the materialistic strand of the American Dream.

There had been a tremendous surge in the number of travelling salesmen employed in the United States at the beginning of the 20th century, when large numbers of new firms were set up by enterprising manufacturers of business machines, domestic appliances, new foodstuffs and pharmaceutical goods. Firms such as Eastman Kodak, Coca-Cola, Westinghouse Electric, Carnegie Steel, Wrigley's Chewing Gum, General Electric and PepsiCo often hired salesmen by the hundreds, or even thousands, to cater to established customers and to create new markets for their products. Since the 1920s, this type of 'sales management' had become a part of all forward-looking manufacturing businesses and good 'salesmanship' was seen as an integral component of 'modern' business models.

Salesmanship flourished as a career opportunity. The job did not demand academic qualifications, but it did demand the ability to charm and, of course, to sell. Willy's credo of **'Be liked and you will never want'** (*Act One*) may not apply to many walks of life, but in sales being liked is a critical ingredient to success. Most travelling salesmen would begin their career on a 'commission only' basis before being moved onto the salaried staff once they had demonstrated their abilities to their employers. Many young men saw a career in sales as a pathway to personal success and many a salesman started their journey to becoming CEO of their own company selling the goods of others 'on the road'.

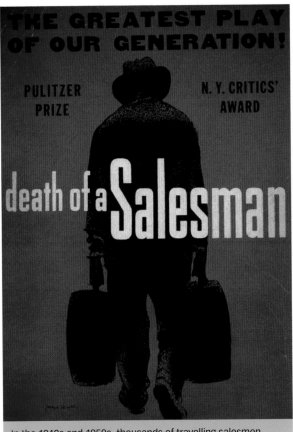

THE GREATEST PLAY OF OUR GENERATION!

PULITZER PRIZE

N. Y. CRITICS' AWARD

death of a **Salesman**

In the 1940s and 1950s, thousands of travelling salesmen spent most of their lives on the road, trying to make a living in difficult circumstances

As part of an organized sales force, salesmen's routes were planned at head office, where sales managers at large corporations assigned their salesmen specific territories and gave them monthly or weekly quotas to meet. Sales workers performed a range of different tasks: explaining and sometimes servicing products, collecting information and pressuring people to make purchases by overcoming any resistance. Salesmen learned to answer specific questions about a product and its application, and to grant credit to buyers and make arrangements for delivery.

Salesmen were also expected to persuade customers to buy products or services that they might not have otherwise purchased. They were particularly valued for introducing new products to customers and persuading them that they needed them. They were also expected to persuade customers to buy their company's product rather than a competitor's, for example, championing a General Electric refrigerator rather than a Hastings.

Willy Loman makes his living as a travelling salesman, but Miller does not disclose what product he sells. We know he carries samples in his bags, so we can assume that the goods are small and portable. Willy has had dreams of starting a business of his own and giving up travelling for ever, but these dreams have come to nothing and, by the time we meet him, his best years are behind him, his salary has been stopped, he has been reduced to a 'commission only' contract once more, **'like a beginner, an unknown'** as Linda describes him (*Act One*), and he is just about surviving, financially, by taking hand-outs from Charley.

Though Biff denounces Willy's employers as **'Those ungrateful bastards'** (*Act One*), Miller is keen to show Howard, Willy's boss and owner of the firm that he works for, as a family man who is simply running his company on strict business principles.

For Willy, the career he had hoped would lead on to greater things has actually had a diminishing effect and he is crushed by his failure to realize his potential as a salesman.

The quest for riches: speculation in gold, diamonds and timber

Like Willy, his father was also a traveller and a salesman. He made and sold flutes for a living, travelling from state to state and crossing the country by wagon, sometimes with the whole family in the back. Eventually, he appears to have given up selling flutes, abandoning his wife and baby son and travelling to Alaska, no doubt hoping to join the 'gold rush' there and become rich. Although Willy's father has not returned to the family a rich man (or indeed at all), his speculative nature is evidently shared by Willy's older brother, Ben.

In the 19th century, enterprising Americans of all ages, inspired by the pioneering spirit, left their homes in their thousands and travelled hundreds of miles when rumours of the discovery of gold in California reached them. This first American 'gold rush' was in 1849, attracting tens of thousands of American and foreign prospectors, who hoped to become rich. Many did strike gold and made their fortunes.

Later, the Alaskan 'gold rush' occurred when gold was discovered in Klondike in 1896 after prospectors had been searching and panning for gold for over 15 years. It is to Alaska that Willy's father goes, in search of his fortune.

Ben attempts to follow him but, due to what he describes as his **'faulty view of geography'** (*Act One*), he finds himself in Africa. While prospectors were panning for gold in America, the discovery of diamonds in South Africa, near the Vaal River, triggered a 'diamond rush' that attracted people from all over the world to Kimberley, at the epicentre of the diamond mines. This is where Ben finds himself.

One of Kimberley's most famous prospectors was Cecil Rhodes, who arrived in South Africa, aged 16, and quickly gained control over many of the region's diamond mines through his De Beers Consolidated Company. Rhodes' story of rapid and fabulous financial success is very similar to the one told by Ben in his first appearance in Act One when he reports how he walked **'into the jungle'** at age 17 and comes out **'rich'**, making his fortune from **'diamond mines'**.

When Ben materializes again in Act Two, he is en route to Alaska where he has bought timberland – not as precious as gold or diamonds but, nevertheless, a very profitable commodity. He offers Willy a position looking after **'things for me'**. Although Willy is tempted by the prospect, excitedly responding, **'God, timberland! Me and my boys in those grand outdoors'**, the younger Linda dismisses the project vigorously, asking rhetorically, **'Why must everybody conquer the world?'** and effectively crushing whatever pioneering spirit Willy possesses.

Miller reflects upon two competing aspects of the American Dream. One is the dream of riches procured through speculation, the pioneering spirit, and good luck as a prospector for treasure in distant parts. Ben is shown to have achieved this dream while Willy's father has disappeared in his quest for it. The other is the dream of social advancement, achieving security for one's family through hard work, perseverance and the teaching of a solid work ethic to one's children. Though Willy has pursued this dream, it has eluded him.

We hear nothing of the lives or ambitions of Ben's seven sons back in Africa, but Willy's sons represent the two competing aspects of the 'dream'. Biff loves the great outdoors but he is torn between the idea of borrowing money to buy a cattle ranch with the possibility of striking oil (speculation) and the consciousness that Willy has planted in him that he **'oughta be makin' my future'** in a more conventional 'white collar' job, like merchandising (*Act One*). He criticizes his father for having **'the wrong dreams'** (*Requiem*). Hap is following in the footsteps of Willy. He spends his days in what Biff describes as **'a measly manner of existence'** (*Act One*), working as **'one of the two assistants to the assistant'** buyer in a store (*Act Two*). He refuses to accept Biff's condemnation of Willy's life, defending Willy's 'dream' as **'the only dream you can have – to come out number-one man'** and he pledges to pursue that dream and **'win it for him'** (*Requiem*).

Miller invites the audience to make a judgement between the life choices made by Willy and Ben, and perpetuated by Biff and Happy, in pursuit of personal fulfilment.

Activity 3

a) What do you learn from *Death of a Salesman* about the value of each model (speculation or dedicated hard work) for achieving success? Draw up a grid showing the pros and cons of each.

b) Now plan an answer to the question: How far do you agree with Biff's verdict on his father that **'He had the wrong dreams'** (*Requiem*)?

Theatrical context

Dramatists

In the 1930s and 1940s, American theatre was enjoying something of a 'golden age'. Despite the competition from cinema in the realm of popular entertainment, this period saw the emergence of four major playwrights, all of whom challenged the dramatic conventions of the time with 'serious' yet popular plays that ushered in one of the most successful periods in American theatre history.

Those four playwrights were Eugene O'Neill (1888–1953), Thornton Wilder (1897–1975), Tennessee Williams (1911–1983) and Arthur Miller (1915–2005).

Eugene O'Neill was a ground-breaking dramatist who is credited with transforming American theatre from a form dominated by melodrama and hackneyed plots to one that focused more on the inner drama of his characters, rather than their physical or social world. He was influenced strongly by theatrical innovations in Europe and, in particular, by Shaw, Ibsen and Strindberg. O'Neill's extensive catalogue of works include *The Hairy Ape* (1921*), Mourning becomes Electra* (1930), *The Iceman Cometh* (1940) and the epic *Long Day's Journey into Night'* (1941), all of which contributed to his international reputation as a theatrical innovator.

Thornton Wilder's best-known play, *Our Town* (1938) opens on a stage with 'No Curtains. No Scenery' and with the 'Stage Manager's' direct address to the audience, introducing them to 'Grover's Corners', a fictional town intended to represent 'every' town in America. The character of the Stage Manager functions like a Greek Chorus, assuming control over the onstage action through **meta-theatrical** devices, including prompting actors and cueing scene changes.

Both Wilder's and O'Neill's work became a direct source of inspiration to his fellow Americans, Tennessee Williams and Arthur Miller, who, each in their different ways, continued the trend of experiment within their stage-craft.

Tennessee Williams' career took off shortly before Miller's and they each had tremendous artistic and commercial successes. Both worked with the inspirational director Elia Kazan, transforming the theatrical landscape with their highly original and varied dramatic output.

Williams first won critical acclaim in 1944 when *The Glass Menagerie* opened in Chicago. *A Streetcar Named Desire* followed in 1947, the same year that Miller had his first theatrical success with *All My Sons*. Williams' plays won many prizes, including the Pulitzer Prize. His success continued with *The Rose Tattoo* (1950), *Cat on a Hot Tin Roof* (1955) and *Sweet Bird of Youth* (1956).

Like Miller, Williams incorporated expressionism into his plays and in *The Glass Menagerie*, in particular, he creates a blending of unfolding memories with a sense of realistic action. Williams is considered to be a more poetical dramatist than Miller, using symbolism freely within his dramas, irrespective of the realistic nature of the plots that he dramatized.

> **meta-theatre** a form of theatre that draws attention to its own theatricality, e.g. when a narrator or Chorus figure steps outside the action to address the audience

The Group Theatre and the Actors Studio

Another significant aspect of the theatrical context of the time was the development of theatrical associations dedicated to training actors in the art of creating convincing psychologically plausible characters.

The late 19th- and early 20th-century American stage had been dominated by popular forms of drama such as melodrama and farce, where the focus was on telling a gripping story or inducing laughter through exaggerated characterization. The 'serious' and more psychologically truthful plays created by dramatists such as Miller and Williams required a more subtle approach to role.

The Group Theatre was founded in 1931 by Harold Clurman, Cheryl Crawford and Lee Strasberg. It was a pioneering attempt to create a company of players trained in a unified style and dedicated to promoting plays with a social message.

Lee J. Cobb, an actor in the Group Theatre, received international acclaim for his performance of Willy Loman both on the American stage and on screen.

At the Group Theatre, and later at the Actors' Studio, Lee Strasberg developed the blueprint for **'method acting'** from Stanislavski's teachings on acting, called 'the system'. Strasberg's 'method' was a collection of training and rehearsal exercises for actors, which taught them to base their performances upon inner emotional experience, uncovered largely through the medium of **improvisation**.

improvisation in theatre, the creation of dramatic scenes without written dialogue and with no predetermined scenario; actors draw on their imaginations to create episodes of action to generate original drama or to explore aspects of characters

method acting a painstaking approach to acting based on a system evolved by Constantin Stanislavski in the early 20th century; it provides actors with methods for utilizing aspects of their own character and experiences to create a role

Psychological realism

The Group Theatre disbanded in 1941 but its ethic was revived in 1947 by the founding of the Actors Studio by Elia Kazan (the director who produced both Williams' and Miller's early plays), Cheryl Crawford and Robert Lewis. The Actors' Studio was also dedicated specifically to the training of actors.

Strasberg became a key figure in this enterprise. Still teaching the 'method' approach to acting, Strasberg and colleague Stella Adler introduced a whole generation of stage and screen actors to an intensive approach to character building. Famous actors such as Paul Newman, Marlon Brando, Al Pacino, Robert De Niro and Dustin Hoffman were all trained using the 'method' approach, as was Marilyn Monroe.

The significance of these theatrical collectives was that they elevated the art of 'acting' into a highly respected art form and furnished the actors who enrolled with the skills to apply a detailed and psychologically credible approach to characterization. It produced a cadre of actors capable of interpreting the complex roles that playwrights such as Miller, Tennessee Williams and others created in their plays.

Writing about context

Understanding how the context of the play may have shaped its creation and development will help you to write with more insight into the text. Remember that you should never attempt to 'shoehorn' contextual facts into your assessment just for the sake of it. Instead, use relevant information to support and enhance your ideas. Contextual information that might be relevant in your assessment could include:

- the Great Depression and post-war America
- the American Dream
- the growth of selling as a career
- the context of speculation for quick financial rewards
- the training of actors in psychologically realistic acting.

Genre

Much of the drama written in the 20th century defies rigid generic classification. Playwrights have experimented with genre as much as they have experimented with dramatic language and form. In *Death of a Salesman*, Miller mixes the dramatic forms of realism and expressionism, and he blends some aspects of the ancient genre of Greek tragedy and its more contemporary variants with the more fluid and modern genre of the memory play.

Tragedy and *Death of a Salesman*

In the weeks, months and years that followed the first production of *Death of a Salesman*, considerable controversy raged about whether or not the play could be considered to be a tragedy. In particular, there was debate over whether or not the play could be regarded as tragic in the Aristotelian sense, as discussed in the section on structure (page 17).

All classical Greek tragedies follow a similar pattern and present the fall of a great man (the **tragic hero**), who falls from greatness to misery because of a **tragic flaw**. His journey from greatness to misery also involves setbacks and reversals of fortune, which build to a climax and end in **catastrophe** for him. At this point, the tragic hero experiences a **tragic recognition** of his circumstances. To be truly tragic, the fall of the hero must have wider implications, affecting the whole state – or society.

Of great importance, in the Aristotelian model of tragedy, is the intended experience of **catharsis** for the audience at the end of the play. The audience is expected to undergo a powerful purging of the emotions of pity (for the defeated **protagonist**) and fear (lest we should meet a similarly tragic ending).

> **catastrophe** in Greek tragedy, the concluding part of the play where the protagonist accepts ruin
>
> **catharsis** the intended audience experience at the end of the tragedy, purging them of the twin emotions of pity and fear
>
> **protagonist** the main character
>
> **tragic flaw (hamartia)** a character fault that leads to the hero's downfall
>
> **tragic hero** the main character, who falls from greatness to misery because of a character flaw
>
> **tragic recognition (anagnorisis)** recognition that the tragedy has been self-inflicted

There has been much discussion about whether or not Miller's story of an ordinary man, a failure in his own eyes and with little capacity for tragic recognition, can be considered to be a tragedy at all, but the general consensus is that Miller adapted the tragic form to create a modern American tragedy.

In the Greek tragedy *Oedipus Rex*, written by Sophocles and first performed around 429 BC, King Oedipus gouges out his own eyes in despair at having killed his father and married his mother

Miller himself has written articles defending the play from those who suggested that Willy Loman is simply too pathetic and insignificant a character to be a tragic hero and Miller's arguments are very persuasive. Certainly, in his essay 'Tragedy and the Common Man', which he wrote at the time of the first production, Miller seems to be putting in a claim for Willy Loman as a tragic figure with whom ordinary theatre-goers can empathize:

 I believe that the common man is as apt a subject for tragedy in its highest sense as kings were.

(Arthur Miller, quoted in *The Theatre Essays of Arthur Miller,* edited by Robert A. Martin, 1978)

I think the tragic feeling is evoked in us when we are in the presence of a character who is ready to lay down his life, if need be, to secure one thing – his sense of personal dignity. From Orestes to Hamlet, Medea to Macbeth, the underlying struggle is that of the individual attempting to gain his 'rightful' position in his society.

(Arthur Miller, as above)

Miller also points to the fact that Greek tragedies were written at a time when society was comprised of 'great men', 'women' and 'slaves', and suggests that in such a context audiences would only be engaged by the dramatizing of the great men as the slaves were of no interest to them.

 Activity 1

a) Consider Miller's definition of the 'tragic feeling' and look for evidence in *Death of a Salesman* where Willy appears to be seeking his 'rightful' position in society.

b) Explain why Miller thinks that Willy is an acceptable tragic hero. Do you agree that Willy lays down his life to secure his dignity?

Tips for assessment

When writing about genre, remember to include elements of the play that don't conform to a particular genre as well as those that do.

Definitions of tragedy that refer to classical Greek models have been applied to a continuously evolving form of tragedy through the ages and across Western theatre. Indeed, every age has produced variants on the tragic form.

In the ancient world and particularly for the Greeks, tragic heroes owed their fates as much to the will of the gods as to their inner flaws. By the time Arthur Miller was writing, tragedy, as a genre, was impossible to conceive of as being in any way the result of the will of the gods or of a single deity. Willy Loman is not a victim of fate but of his personal struggle to succeed in a world where failure is not tolerated – the world of the American dream.

If Miller's play is accepted as being a modern tragedy, the most significant aspect of its tragic form is the dramatic journey of Willy Loman, which might be considered to parallel, to a certain extent, the journey of the protagonist in classical Greek theatre (as defined above), conferring the status of tragic hero upon Willy.

Activity 2

Do you agree that Willy Loman fits the definition of tragic hero as understood by the Greeks or as defined by Miller? Look back through the play and identify the moments where Willy:

- is in some way 'great'
- is considered to be a hero by others
- falls from greatness (identify his tragic flaw as well as what he does to prompt the fall)
- recognizes his self-inflicted tragedy
- accepts ruin/catastrophe

or simply:

- struggles 'to gain his "rightful" position in his society'.

Write the opening paragraph of an answer to the question above, indicating whether or not you agree that Willy could be defined as a tragic hero.

The memory play

The term 'memory play' refers to drama in which memory plays a key part in the experience of the protagonist. The term is used to describe a genre of theatre based either on the re-constructed memories of the playwright or on the completely invented memories of the protagonist in the play. The term was first coined by Tennessee Williams.

Rather than referring to memory as a theme in his drama as, for example, Shakespeare does in *Hamlet*, Williams used it as a structural device, translating the inner workings of the mind into a form of dramatic expression. In the stage directions for *The Glass Menagerie* (1944), Williams states: *'The scene is memory and is therefore non-realistic. Memory takes a lot of poetic licence. It omits some details; others are exaggerated.'* The character Tom Wingfield, who represents Williams in the play, speaks directly to the audience from the outset, telling them, 'The play is memory. Being a memory play, it is dimly lighted, it is sentimental, it is not realistic.' The play is punctuated with Tom's one-sided 'conversations' with the audience as he looks back on his life.

Miller admired Williams' treatment of memory in *The Glass Menagerie* but his own version of the memory play genre in *Death of a Salesman* is entirely different. In the first place, there is no narrator to mediate between the actors and the audience. Instead, Willy's memories absorb him in his present state and are peopled by the phantoms of his imagination, acting out scenes from his remembered or reinvented past.

Miller explained his innovative use of memory as a device in the play in his *Introduction to the Collected Plays*, published in 1957:

> There are no flashbacks in this play but only a mobile concurrency of past and present, and this, again, because in his desperation to justify his life Willy Loman has destroyed the boundaries between now and then…
>
> (Arthur Miller, quoted in *The Theatre Essays of Arthur Miller*, edited by Robert A. Martin, 1978)

It is this 'concurrency' of events past and present that makes Miller's use of the memory play genre so dramatically effective.

Willy's memories are involuntary; they overwhelm him when incidents in the present remind him of the past. For example, in Act One his mention to Linda of the **'red Chevvy'** that he owned in 1928 unlocks his memories of Biff and Happy polishing the car when they were teenagers, before his relationship with Biff is soured.

Later, within the same memory sequence in Act One, Linda's reassurance that Willy is **'the handsomest'** of men sparks Willy's darker memory of the Woman's laughter. Willy then becomes completely immersed in the guilty memory of his adulterous liaison in response to Linda's comment that **'Few men are idolized by their children the way you are'** *(Act One)*.

In this way, Miller presents a series of memories crowding in upon Willy, from different moments in his past, while the character of Willy remains, for the audience, permanently in the present.

Realism

Realism is a style of theatre that depends upon an appearance of real life being presented on stage. In realistic drama, the audience looks into a room or sees a recognizable location from 'real' life. Action takes place chronologically and characters interact using dialogue that mirrors natural speech. The play proceeds logically from the initial situation presented, through a series of developments or complications, to the final denouement where the story comes to a fitting conclusion, either resolving issues satisfactorily for the main character(s) or concluding unhappily.

Activity 3

Which hallmarks of realism are present in *Death of a Salesman*? Which hallmarks are not present?

Social realism

Following on from his first successful drama, *All My Sons, Death of a Salesman* helped to secure Miller's reputation as a social dramatist and many critics consider both plays to belong to the sub-genre of social realism.

Miller himself makes a claim for viewing the play as **social realism** in two of the theatre essays that he wrote in the 1950s, 'On social plays' (1958) and 'The family in modern drama' (1959). In 'On social plays', Miller suggests that modern drama needs to do more than simply analyse the network of relationships within society but that it should 'delve into the nature of man as he exists to discover what his needs are, so that those needs be amplified and exteriorized in terms of social concepts' (*The Theatre Essays of Arthur Miller*, edited by Robert A. Martin, 1978).

> **social realism** a genre that adopts a realistic approach and focuses on everyday life; usually on the working classes, the poor or the destitute, the work encompasses a critique of dominant social structures

Expressionism

Expressionism is a particularly difficult genre to define as it covers a wide range of different cultural manifestations, both in art and in literature.

The movement was originally artistic and may be described as an art form in which exaggeration or distortion of surface reality is used to depict an inner truth. Expressionist drama emerged in Germany in the early 20th century. The two German expressionist playwrights who had the most influence on the development of this non-naturalistic style of drama in Europe and America were George Kaiser (1878–1945) and Ernst Toller (1893–1939).

This distinctive theatrical style had the following key features:

- **Focus** These are plays of protest and rebellion, both against society and the status quo, and against naturalistic forms of drama. Many early expressionist plays decry the older generation and call upon 'death' to fathers.
- **Settings** are often abstract or dream-like and unlocalized, with no attempt at dramatic illusion. Props are sparse and/or symbolic.
- **Action** of the play is episodic, often representing stages in the protagonist's life or a series of 'visions' as if filtered through his subconscious mind.
- **Characters** remain nameless or representative of a role or function in society, e.g. the Son, the Mother, the Supervisor.
- **Crowd scenes** involve robotic movement and anonymous performers.
- **Dialogue** is often reduced to what has been described as 'telegram' style; clipped speech rhythms alternate with extended 'rhapsodic' monologues.
- **Style of acting** is often declamatory and/or expressive of intense emotion.

Only a selection of these features were embraced and/or adapted by the American playwrights Elmer Rice, Eugene O'Neill, Tennessee Williams and Arthur Miller.

Although *Death of a Salesman* does not conform fully to an expressionist model, there are certainly aspects both in its staging and in its characterization that can be traced to an expressionist influence.

It is clear from Miller's original title of the play – *The Inside of His Head* – that he was not slavishly following a *realistic* model in his approach to *Death of a Salesman*. Instead, he had envisaged a setting that would consist of an enormous face the height of the **proscenium arch**, which would appear and then open up, revealing the inside of a man's head. Such a setting would certainly have been expressionistic. Miller later abandoned both the title and the proposed setting. However, in the first production, the director, designer and composer found a way of creating a set that reflected both the realistic and the expressionistic forms that Miller blends in the lengthy stage directions that open the play.

> **proscenium arch** the often arched structure over the stage that is part of the structure of the theatre and not part of the stage set

See the table below for ways in which *Death of a Salesman* reflects aspects of expressionism.

Expressionist feature	Reflected in *Death of a Salesman*
Plays of protest against society, the older generation and the family; fathers	• Critique of the American Dream • Critique of the nuclear family • The expectations of Willy and Linda are shown to be responsible for the sense of discontent/inadequacy experienced by both Biff and Happy
Settings are dream-like and abstract	• Although the setting is semi-realistic, it is sparse; props and furnishings are used symbolically • During 'memory' scenes, entrances and exits cut across designated 'doors' and 'walls', and locations are transformed in Willy's imagination, e.g. the washroom in the restaurant becomes the setting for the hotel room in Boston
Characters are nameless or represent a function in society or an abstract quality (like Power or Violence)	• Although Miller gives his characters names, Willy and Linda represent husband/wife, father/mother, and both Biff and Happy can be seen as aspects of Willy's personality, representing competing models of the American Dream • In a fully expressionistic reading of the play, one could imagine the cast list as: Father, Mother, Elder Son, Younger Son, Neighbour, Neighbour's Son, Employer, 'Woman' • It would also be possible to categorize the roles of Willy and Linda as representing abstractions such as Anxiety and Patience
Crowd scenes	Not applicable
Dialogue: telegram style/ rhapsodic monologue	Miller does not adopt the telegram style in the dialogue although there are a number of set-piece speeches that might be described as rhapsodic, e.g. Biff's speech about 'wasting' his life in Act One, Linda's **'Attention must be paid'** speech and Willy's speech to Howard about Dave Singleman
Exaggerated acting style	This will vary from production to production but Miller has not written the dialogue to be exaggerated in an expressionistic style

Activity 4

Using the table above to help you, write a paragraph about each of the members of the Loman family, explaining how their expressionistic function sheds light on how Miller wants us to understand their characters.

Absurdism

Despite Arthur Miller's confession that when he wrote *Death of a Salesman* he often found himself laughing out loud, few commentators have discerned many elements of comedy in Willy's final 24 hours.

Of course, Willy does contradict himself – especially at the beginning of Act One – in ways that some readers/audiences find amusing. For example, first he describes Biff as **'a lazy bum'** and then within a few lines he assures Linda that **'There's one thing about Biff – he's not lazy'**. He has a similarly mercurial change of mind about his Chevrolet, first describing it to Linda in Act One as **'the greatest car ever built'** but almost immediately declaring, **'That goddam Chevrolet, they ought to prohibit the manufacture of that car'** when he learns how much it is costing him.

These elements of contradiction have been read by some as being features of the genre of absurdism, which evolved more fully, both in America and in Europe, in the 1950s and 60s. Elements of the play that anticipate the Absurdist movement include:

- the non-naturalistic, 'symbolic' set, especially as it was originally conceived as the interior of a skull
- the fractured time structure
- the use of non-rational events, such as the manifestation of Ben
- the disruption of language and meaning, as evidenced in Willy's contradictions, exaggerations and rants
- the lack of a dramatic resolution, as Hap prepares to perpetuate the dream that has been exposed as futile.

The *Death of a Salesman* does not fall neatly into any one dramatic genre but its success may in part be the result of Miller's fusion of a range of generic elements.

Writing about genre

In your assessment, you may be asked to comment on the theatrical genre(s) of *Death of a Salesman*. Remember that it is not clear cut and that you may need to discuss how Miller blends different generic elements within the play. When writing about the genre of the play, make sure that you:

- Write about the drama as a construct (i.e. an artistically constructed world is being depicted on stage) about created characters, not as if it is about the lives of real people.
- Use the correct terminology, such as 'tragedy' or 'memory play'.
- Show that you are aware of the shifting tones between optimism and pessimism.
- Be aware of the different ways in which the play can be interpreted; not all commentators see Willy Loman as a tragic hero, for example.
- Bring your understanding of genre to bear on your analysis of individual aspects of the play, such as its frenetic build-up to the climax of the tragedy in Act Two.

Characterization and Roles

One of the challenges of writing about Miller's presentation of the Loman family, and of Charley and Bernard, is that these characters are seen objectively in the present but, at other times, they are shown as filtered through Willy's perceptions and memories of the past.

Of the other characters, Howard, Charley's secretary, Jenny, the Waiters and two girls at the Chop House only feature in the present, while Ben and the Woman exist in the past and in Willy's mind.

Main characters

Willy Loman

It is useful to consider Willy's characterization in relation to the various roles that he plays in his life – as a son, husband, father, neighbour, brother, lover and employee. These different roles help to define Willy Loman in his struggle to understand his own identity and to accept his worth.

Although Miller suggests, through the title of the play, that Willy Loman is defined by his role as a salesman, we never actually see him working in that capacity in the play.

> **Activity 1**
>
> Write a paragraph explaining why you think Miller chose not to depict Willy at work.

Willy as a husband

We see Willy first as a husband, returning unexpectedly from an aborted sales trip. Although he attempts to reassure Linda that **'It's all right'** and is concerned that she shouldn't be **'worried about me'** *(Act One)*, Miller is quick to establish the inequality in the marital relationship and to reveal Willy as the family patriarch, through Linda's exaggerated deference to him, as demonstrated through the stage directions.

> **Key quotation**
>
> *... she more than loves him, she admires him, as though his mercurial nature, his temper, his massive dreams and little cruelties, served her only as sharp reminders of the turbulent longings within him...*
> *(Act One)*

In his happy memories, Willy shows a gallant attitude towards his wife, insisting that the boys help her with the washing, confiding in her about his feelings of insecurity, and expressing his devotion to her: **'You're the best there is, Linda'** *(Act One)*. In short, he shows a dependence upon her that is absent in the scenes in the present, in Act One, where he shouts at her for buying the 'wrong' cheese and savagely excludes her from his interaction with their sons, as they anticipate the success of Loman Brothers.

Linda loves and admires Willy, who treats her very gallantly and with devotion, at least in his memories; from the 2015 Royal Shakespeare Company production, starring Antony Sher as Willy and Harriet Walters as Linda

Later, we discover that Willy's guilt over his affair with the Woman torments him. He admits to both Biff and Ben that Linda 'has suffered' *(Act Two)*. However, he justifies his affair to himself in Act One by telling Linda, 'I get so lonely' *(Act One)*. Willy's greater betrayal of Linda is his suicide. His misguided belief in Act Two that he is 'worth more dead than alive' robs Linda of any contentment that might have been her due in old age, consigning her to terrible loneliness.

Willy as a father

Willy's experience as a son is shown to have influenced his behaviour as a father and it is his role as a father that is his most significant in the play. As a son, he was abandoned by his 'wild-hearted' father and his only memory of him is of 'a man with a big beard' *(Act One)*. His father left the family to search for his fortune in the Alaskan 'gold rush', but never returned, leaving Willy still feeling 'kind of temporary about myself' *(Act One)*.

As a result of this, Willy has striven to be a good father to Biff and Happy, and is shown to be perpetually anxious about whether or not he has brought them up properly. Although the phantasm Ben assures Willy that he is 'being first-rate with your boys' and that they are 'Outstanding, manly chaps' *(Act One)*, Miller shows them to be something very different. Linda refers to them as 'a pair of animals' *(Act Two)*, calling Happy a 'philandering bum' and dismissing Biff, at 34, as nothing more than 'a boy' *(Act One)*. Miller's implication is that this is as a result of being fed the wrong dreams by Willy. In an attempt to be a good father, Willy has a range of mottos or mantras that he uses to instil good values into his sons, but 'boiled down' they are fairly trite precepts for happiness or success.

Key quotations

Never leave a job till you're finished – remember that.
(Willy, Act One)

Be liked and you will never want.
(Willy, Act One)

Everybody likes a kidder, but nobody lends him money.
(Willy, Act One)

It's not what you say, it's how you say it – because personality always wins the day.
(Willy, Act One)

Willy has adopted the values of his brother Ben, who has made the pursuit of riches his life's goal and appears to measure both happiness and success in material terms. By passing on these values to his sons, Willy has done them both harm.

Willy's fractured relationships with his adult sons are shown to be the result of his own behaviour. His blatant favouritism of Biff over Happy is present in both the scenes set in the present and in the past.

Happy's announcements, in the present, in each act, about intending to be married are effectively ignored by both Willy and Linda, as they focus their attention on Biff. Even in Willy's happy memories of the boys, when Hap desperately tries to gain his father's approval about losing weight, Willy either disregards or belittles him. However, Biff's relationship with Willy has been destroyed by the discovery of 'the Woman' in Willy's hotel room.

Willy's failure as a father is more destructive to his self-esteem than his failure as a salesman. His decision to kill himself, to benefit Biff principally, confirms Linda's claim that Willy loved his sons **'better than his life'** *(Act One)*. Willy turns his death into an act of self-sacrifice, and almost celebration, rather than one of despair.

Key quotation

Oh, Ben, I always knew one way or another we were gonna make it, Biff and I!

(Willy, Act Two)

Willy as a brother

Willy's role as a brother is also significant. He is the hero-worshipping younger brother who tries to impress his successful sibling while tolerating his often contemptuous attitude. Although Ben is a figment of Willy's imagination, he rarely misses an opportunity to be disparaging about Willy's career and achievement. Willy assiduously ignores these slights and continues to treasure and act on Ben's advice. Ben's approval of Willy's scheme to kill himself to secure Biff's future, as **'A perfect proposition all around'**, seals Willy's fate *(Act Two)*.

Willy's relationship with Ben is based on a model of fraternal rivalry that Willy can never hope to win. Where Willy is domesticated, Ben is the great adventurer. Willy's financial security is precarious, whereas Ben is fabulously wealthy. Willy is steady and cautious, while Ben is reckless and a risk-taker. Miller presents Willy's character by comparing him, as Willy compares himself, with the successful, if fantastical, elder brother.

Activity 2

Compare Miller's presentation of the relationship between brothers Willy and Ben with that of brothers Happy and Biff. Think about the similarities and differences between these significant relationships. You might like to present your ideas in a table.

Willy as a neighbour

As a neighbour, Willy appears churlish and ungrateful. It is obvious that Willy's hostility towards his good neighbour is engendered by jealousy of his success.

> **Key quotation**
>
> You been jealous of me all your life, you damned fool!
> *(Charley, Act One)*

The line above is delivered, however, as Charley counts out the 110 dollars that Willy has asked for in order to pay his insurance. Despite taking handouts from Charley, Willy never stops abusing him. When Charley comes to play cards, to calm Willy down, in Act One, Willy ends up accusing him of cheating. He also calls him 'disgusting' for not being able to 'handle tools'. It seems that Willy consoles himself for not being as successful as Charley by belittling his neighbour, calling him an 'ignoramus' even when Charley is trying to help him *(Act Two)*. Miller reveals this to be a most unattractive quality in Willy.

Finally, after he has lost his job, Willy acknowledges that Charley is 'the only friend I got' and he congratulates him on Bernard's evident success, telling him, 'He's a fine boy' *(Act Two)*. Unable to relinquish his dream for his own sons, he adds, 'They're all fine boys, and they'll end up big – all of them' as he anticipates Biff and Happy becoming rich and successful as Loman Brothers, another delusion that will be smashed before the end of the play.

Willy as a lover

We only see Willy in his role of lover through his own memory. The first time he remembers the Woman, in Act One, he sees himself in a flattering light. The Woman tells him emphatically that she 'picked' him, that Willy is good for her and that she thinks he is 'a wonderful man'. Willy recalls the compliments that she paid him: 'you're so sweet. And such a kidder' *(Act One)*. He remembers the stockings he gave her as a sign of his generosity as a lover, but Miller is also inviting us to compare the 'lot of stockings' that the Woman has from Willy with Linda's need to mend hers; as she says, 'They're so expensive' *(Act One)*.

In the Woman's second appearance, Willy's treatment of her is disgraceful. Faced with the exposure of his affair, Willy bundles her out of the hotel room only half dressed. The stage directions describe her as both *'angry'* and *'humiliated'* (Act Two); Willy's memory reveals him to have been unchivalrous and unfeeling as a lover.

Willy as an employee

When Willy confronts his employer about working in New York, Miller shows us an employee who has not been able to adapt to having a boss the same age as his sons. Rather than treating Howard with due respect, he patronizes him by reminding him that he was only a baby when Willy was a successful salesman with the firm.

Willy monopolizes Howard's time with his anecdote about Dave Singleman and when this story fails to impress Howard, Willy yells at him.

> **Key quotation**
>
> I put thirty-four years into this firm, Howard, and now I can't pay my insurance! You can't eat the orange and throw the peel away – a man is not a piece of fruit!
> *(Willy, Act Two)*

This eloquent and impassioned plea dignifies Willy in the eyes of the audience but does not sway Howard at all. Howard fires Willy and this results in a loss of identity for the salesman and certainly contributes to his decision to kill himself.

Willy is the play's central character. As the father figure, Willy plays a large part in any expressionist reading of the play. He is also, arguably, the tragic hero of the play.

Willy is associated with themes of identity, family relationships, material success, the American Dream, loyalty and betrayal, lies and illusions, memory.

Linda

Early in the play, Willy describes Linda as **'my foundation and my support'** *(Act One)*. Linda supports Willy throughout the real-time action of the play, defending him to his sons and shielding him from their disapproval. She is as much a mother figure to Willy as she is a wife, fussing over him when he returns from Yonkers, tolerating his changeable moods, soothing him to sleep with her humming.

In Act Two, Linda becomes more fiercely protective of Willy, to the extent of ordering the boys out of the house for deserting Willy in the Chop House. Miller presents Linda as a patient and undemanding wife, who consistently boosts Willy's confidence, overlooks his short temper and allows him to maintain the fiction that he is still earning some money.

Although Miller shows us that the boys both love their mother, as Biff refers to her as his **'pal'** and Happy wants to marry someone **'Like Mom, y'know?'** *(Act One)*, Linda's love for Willy far exceeds her feelings for her sons.

> **Key quotation**
>
> Get out of here, both of you, and don't come back! I don't want you tormenting him any more. Go on now, get your things together!
> *(Linda, Act Two)*

Activity 3

Research 'Oedipus complex'. Do you think it could be relevant to the Loman family dynamics? Discuss this in your group.

However, Linda fully appreciates that Willy is a difficult man and she tries to keep the peace between him and Biff, in particular. She suspects that something has happened to disturb the close relationship they once enjoyed but cannot get either of them to reveal what happened. Conscious that some of Willy's problems stem from his uneasiness with Biff, she cautions Willy about criticizing Biff, telling him, **'You mustn't lose your temper with him'** *(Act One)*.

The Linda of the present ignores Willy's outbursts and his put-downs, and tries to accommodate his whims. She is more fatalistic than Willy, functioning as a contrast to him in this regard; she accepts the fact that once the house is paid for, the boys will have left home and she tries to console Willy by reminding him that **'life is a casting off'** *(Act One)*. She functions as a pragmatist to Willy's idealist tendencies.

The phrase 'casting-off' could refer to the domestic activity of knitting, in which 'to cast off' means to finish a garment in such a way as to prevent the unravelling of the stitches. Alternatively, we also associate 'casting off' with the untying of a boat from its mooring before setting off to sea.

The younger Linda of Willy's imagination is naturally more youthful and energetic, and she is also more opinionated. Although proud of Biff the football hero, Linda is not uncritical of his wildness. Nor is she afraid of opposing Ben when he visits Willy and offers him a place looking after his timberland. She is happy with her life as it is and does not want Ben putting ideas into Willy's head about the **'grand outdoors'** *(Act Two)*.

> **Key quotation**
>
> **Enough to be happy right here, right now. [*To Willy, while Ben laughs*]**
> **Why must everyone conquer the world?**
> *(Linda, Act Two)*

It is the younger Linda that Willy is unfaithful to, the younger Linda who must mend her old stockings while Willy gives new stockings to the Woman, and the younger Linda who tells Willy that he is **'The handsomest'** *(Act One)*.

Oblivious to Willy's infidelity, it is the older Linda who urges Biff to be **'sweet'** to his father, who she describes as **'only a little boat looking for a harbour'** *(Act Two)*. Linda's powerful defence of Willy to Biff and Happy in Act One demonstrates her commitment to her husband and also reveals her compassion.

> **Key quotation**
>
> **I don't say he's a great man. Willie Loman never made a lot of money.**
> **His name was never in the paper. He's not the finest character that ever**
> **lived. But he's a human being, and a terrible thing is happening to him.**
> **So attention must be paid. He's not to be allowed to fall in his grave like**
> **an old dog. Attention, attention must be finally paid to such a person.**
> *(Linda, Act One)*

It is the older Linda who is the real victim of Willy's delusions and his suicide. Living on in a house that is paid for but without the man she loved so fiercely, Linda struggles to understand his action and her final cry of **'We're free'** *(Requiem)*, before the curtain falls is poignantly ironic.

Linda functions as a facilitator to Willy's illusions about himself. In an expressionist reading of the play she is the mother figure that the younger generation must oppose. In a psychoanalytical, Oedipal reading, she is desired by both of her sons who seek to displace their father. Feminist critics see her as the archetypal, undervalued wife, associated in Willy's memories with laundry and drudgery.

Linda is associated with themes of the American Dream, loyalty and betrayal, and family secrets.

Biff Loman

Some commentators have suggested that Miller is more interested in Biff than in Willy Loman, but as the play centres on Willy and his perceptions, this is hard to support. Certainly, Biff has more self-awareness than either Willy or Hap, and he functions as Miller's mouthpiece, to some extent, in his criticism of the 'daily grind' and the competitiveness that lies beneath the myth of the American Dream.

> **Key quotation**
>
> Shipping clerk, salesman, business of one kind or another. And it's a measly manner of existence.
> *(Biff, Act One)*

Biff appears in the present and also in Willy's memories and imagination. As the favoured son, he is critical to Willy's emotional and mental well-being. In the sections set in Biff's 'glory days' as a high-school football star, he is depicted as a boy with a golden future. In the sections set in the present, he is a failure in Willy's eyes and consequently a disappointment to himself.

> **Key quotation**
>
> What the hell am I doing, playing around with horses, twenty-eight dollars a week! I'm thirty-four years old, I oughta be makin' my future.
> *(Biff, Act One)*

When Willy remembers Biff in Act One, he remembers the boy who idolized him, who wants to succeed in order to please him and who tells him that he won't be nervous about his big game **'if you're gonna be there'**. It is Biff who absorbs his father's view on life that being **'well liked'** is the key to success and he has cultivated a large group of followers who are happy to **'sweep out the furnace room'** for the privilege of hanging out with Biff Loman *(Act One)*.

Biff's character is shown to be influenced negatively by his father's uncritical appreciation of him. Willy turns a blind eye to Biff's criminal tendencies: he passes off his theft of a football as an example of initiative, he shrugs off Bernard's claim that Biff is **'driving the car without a licence'** and Linda's complaint that Biff is **'too rough with the girls'** *(Act One)*. Not only this, but Willy positively encourages Biff to cheat in the state maths examinations and he boasts to Ben about the value of the materials that the boys have stolen from the building site next door. It is unsurprising that Biff later admits to having been in jail for stealing a suit and having **'stole myself out of every good job since high school'** *(Act Two)*. Miller suggests that Biff is a victim of Willy's hapless parenting style, just as Willy himself was a victim of his father, who abandoned him to search for gold.

Miller also suggests that Biff's future evaporated on the night that he discovered the Woman in his father's hotel room; Willy's status as Biff's 'hero' was downgraded to that of a **'phony little fake'** *(Act Two)*. Later in Act Two, Bernard tells Willy that he believed that Biff had **'given up his life'** after what happened in Boston, although neither Biff not Willy have ever spoken of it to each other or to anyone else.

Activity 4

Who do you think is to blame for Biff's lack of success in life – Biff or Willy? Write a bullet point list of arguments supporting each point of view. Find quotations to support each bullet and explain your conclusion.

While the boy Biff longed to accompany his father on some of his sales trips, carrying Willy's bags and being introduced to the buyers in the Boston store, in Act One the adult Biff scorns the life that depends on a **'measly manner of existence'**, dependent upon **'keeping stock, or making phone calls, or selling or buying'**. If Biff retains any of Willy's allegiance to the notion of the American Dream, it is in its original form of the pioneers with a longing for the great outdoors, for working with one's hands and living off the land.

Ultimately, Biff has an epiphany about himself, suddenly seeing things more clearly after waiting in vain to speak to Bill Oliver. Having stolen Oliver's fountain pen, possibly a symbol both of the business world that he despises and of his name or signature 'Biff Loman', he confesses to his father, **'I am not a leader of men, Willy, and neither are you'** *(Act Two)*.

Key quotation

I'm one dollar an hour, Willy! I tried seven states and couldn't raise it. A buck an hour! Do you gather my meaning? I'm not bringing home any prizes any more, and you're going to stop waiting for me to bring them home!
(Biff, Act Two)

Biff's revelation about himself leads him to try to make his whole family see how deluded they have been, not just about him but about themselves.

Key quotations

I realized what a ridiculous lie my whole life has been. We've been talking in a dream for fifteen years. I was a shipping clerk.
(Biff, Act Two)

We never told the truth for ten minutes in this house!
(Biff, Act Two)

Why am I trying to become what I don't want to be? What am I doing in an office, making a contemptuous, begging fool of myself, when all I want is out there, waiting for me the minute I say I know who I am! Why can't I say that, Willy?
(Biff, Act Two)

Activity 5

Does Biff's realization of his own weakness qualify him for the status of tragic hero of the play? Write two paragraphs that justify this viewpoint.

In Requiem, Biff states his belief that his father **'didn't know who he was'** and that he had all **'the wrong dreams'** *(Requiem)*. He recognizes that what Willy actually enjoyed was working **'with his hands'** *(Requiem)* and that he, Biff, does know himself and shares his father's pleasure in honest labour. Biff has accepted that his future is with **'the things that I love in this world. The work and the food and time to sit and smoke'** *(Act Two)*.

Biff's disillusionment with his father led him to give **'up his life'** *(Act Two)*, but it has also freed him from the kind of **'measly manner of existence'** *(Act One)* that Hap has committed himself to in his unquestioning acceptance of Willy's dreams.

Biff is associated with themes of fathers and sons. In an expressionist reading of the play, Biff is the son that longs to defeat his father and, in an Oedipal reading, to displace his father from his mother's affections.

While Happy accepts Willy's version of the American Dream, Biff realizes that his father had 'the wrong dreams'; from the 2015 Royal Shakespeare Company production

Some critics view him as a co-tragic protagonist because of his epiphany, which is closer to tragic recognition of himself than anything that Willy experiences.

Biff is also linked to themes of sibling rivalry, loyalty and betrayal, family secrets, domestic happiness and the American Dream.

Hap Loman (Happy)

In the stage directions that introduce the first appearance of Biff and Happy, Miller describes Happy as *'tall, powerfully made. Sexuality is like a visible colour on him, or a scent that many women have discovered' (Act One)*. Miller also tells us that Happy is *'lost'* and *'hard-skinned'* but *'confused' (Act One)*, although he appears to be more contented than his brother Biff.

In the course of the play Miller shows Happy to be a great deal like his father. Although not the favourite son, Happy has embraced Willy's dream and projects himself as a confident and successful assistant buyer in a New York store.

Happy's constant pursuit and conquest of women appears to be his main drive in life. His penchant for sleeping with the fiancées of senior colleagues at the store has become something of an obsession, which even he recognizes as *'a crummy characteristic' (Act One)*. 'Crummy', too, is the way Happy lies to seduce the girls he meets. When chatting up Miss Forsythe, who is described as being *'now really impressed' (Act Two)*, for example, he explains that he got the nickname Happy at West Point, America's most prestigious military academy. Biff later exposes Happy's delusions of grandeur, reminding him that he is, in fact, *'one of the two assistants to the assistant'* buyer *(Act Two)*. Another unattractive trait that Miller reveals about Happy is his willingness to take bribes, although he tells Biff that he hates himself for it.

Like Willy, Happy is big on talk and empty gestures. His promise to his father that *'I'm gonna retire you for life'* is shown to be hollow *(Act One)* and, although he takes the credit for giving his parents money at Christmas, Linda reveals how inadequate the gesture was, *'fifty dollars! To fix the hot water it cost ninety-seven fifty!' (Act One)*.

Activity 6

The Woman tells Willy that he is **'the saddest, self-centredest soul I ever did see'** *(Act Two)*. Could this description also be applied to Happy? Make a list of the qualities that Happy shares with Willy.

Miller suggests that, like Biff, Happy had been moulded by his father's expectations. Happy has struggled for the attention of his parents by adopting Willy's dreams. The pursuit of these dreams does not bring him happiness, however, and when Biff asks him if he is **'content'**, he replies with an emphatic **'Hell, no!'**, describing himself as lonely despite **'My own apartment, a car, and plenty of women'** *(Act One)*.

Leaving his father in the washroom of the Chop House in order to pursue 'Strudel' is Happy's lowest point in the audience's eyes *(Act Two)*. He not only abandons him in a state of extreme distress but he denies that Willy is even his father, telling Letta, 'He's just a guy' *(Act Two)*. Happy's denial of Willy as his father has been compared by some commentators to the denial of Christ by his disciple Peter.

In short, although Happy recognizes Biff as a poet and calls him 'an idealist' *(Act One)*, he himself has no such redeeming qualities. He has accepted Willy's world view without question, demeans women and is completely lacking in the self-knowledge that allows Biff, finally, to break out of the cycle of self-loathing and failure, and to recognize his true place in the world. Unlike Biff, by the end of the play, Happy has learned nothing.

> **Key quotation**
>
> I'm gonna show you and everybody else that Willy Loman did not die in vain. He had a good dream. It's the only dream you can have – to come out number-one man. He fought it out here, and this is where I'm gonna win it for him.
> *(Happy, Requiem)*

Happy is associated with the themes of fathers and sons. In an expressionist reading of the play he represents the son figure who feels ambiguous about his father, complying with Willy's dream while actively disrespecting him. In an Oedipal reading he longs for his mother's love and wishes to displace her affection for his father.

Happy is also associated with themes of self-deception, sibling rivalry, the American Dream and the role of women.

Charley and Bernard

Charley is Willy's next-door neighbour, his only friend and functions as a **foil** to Willy. Charley is a successful businessman who has his own office, secretary and accountant. We meet his son Bernard, both in the present and the memory scenes, where he is depicted as a serious and studious young man who is shown to have idolized Biff in his teenage years.

The relationship between Charley and his son Bernard offers an interesting contrast to the father–son relationship that exists between Willy and Biff.

Willy appears to have been jealous of Charley for a long time and he only once appears appreciative of all the things that Charley has done for him. Willy derides Charley, calling him an 'ignoramus' to his face *(Act Two)* and, behind his back, expressing his belief that Charley is 'liked, but he's not – well liked' *(Act One)*.

foil in literature, a character whose characteristics completely contrast with one of the main characters, highlighting the character traits of that main character

Throughout the play, however, Miller shows Charley to be a humane man, who, unlike Willy, is conscious of his own failings. Despite his personal failings – his lack of 'interest in anything' *(Act Two)*, including his own son's education; an inability to 'put up a ceiling' *(Act One)*; and an unsentimental attitude towards life – Charley is shown to be a good man with a fund of common sense. Charley is willing and able to spare money to subsidize Willy, thus protecting him from the shame of admitting to Linda that he is making no money. He repeatedly offers Willy a job and he offers him sound advice, which Willy refuses or is unable to take.

Both Charley and Bernard have seen Willy and his boys at close quarters when the boys were growing up and they both seem to understand that Biff is somehow at the root of Willy's unhappiness. In Act One, when Willy bemoans the fact that Biff is returning to Texas and that Willy is unable to give him anything, Charley tells him to 'Forget about him', adding cynically, 'When a deposit bottle is broken, you don't get your nickel back'. In Act Two Charley's son Bernard also advises Willy to 'walk away' from his problems with Biff; but when Willy asks, 'But if you can't walk away?', Bernard concedes, 'I guess that's when it's tough'.

Miller uses Charley and Bernard to represent a normal and healthy father and son relationship. Bernard has become a lawyer and has a family with two boys of his own but he still drops by to see Charley on his way to Washington.

Activity 7

Plan and then write an essay for this question: 'Analyse the function of the roles of Charley and Bernard in *Death of a Salesman*.'

For each of your paragraphs, include at least one supporting textual reference.

Charley is proud of his son's achievements but neither he nor Bernard brag that he is about to 'argue a case in front of the Supreme Court' *(Act Two)*. When Willy hears this, he is astounded, telling Charley, 'he didn't even mention it', to which he receives the telling reply, 'He don't have to – he's gonna do it'. Neither Charley nor Bernard have to exaggerate stories of their success like the Lomans as both have achieved their potential through hard work and perseverance.

Bernard is depicted as a direct contrast to Biff in the scenes from Willy's memories. Willy laughs at Bernard and calls him a pest when he tries to persuade Biff to study for his maths exam. After he returns to his revision, Willy calls Bernard 'an anaemic' and makes disparaging comparisons between Bernard and his own two 'Adonises' *(Act One)*. In a typically unrealistic assessment of Bernard, Willy assures his sons that although 'Bernard can get the best marks in school, y'understand, but when he gets out in the business world, y'understand, you are going to be five times ahead of him' *(Act One)*, a prediction that is never fulfilled.

It is because Charley has been presented as such a down-to-earth character that his eulogy to Willy, in Requiem, is so touching in its sincerity.

> **Key quotation**
>
> Nobody dast blame this man. You don't understand: Willy was a
> salesman. And for a salesman there is no rock bottom to the life [...]
> A salesman is got to dream, boy. It comes with the territory.
> *(Charley, Requiem)*

Charley and Bernard function as foils to Willy and his sons. They are also related
to the theme of the American Dream. Willy constantly disparages Charley for not
knowing how to use tools, whereas Willy is so good with his hands.

Ben

Ben is Willy's elder brother, who, we learn in Act One, has only recently died. Perhaps
Miller intends the audience to deduce that this is why Ben is at the forefront of
Willy's mind. Ben comes to dominate Willy's imagination and, especially in the closing
moments of Act Two, to guide him to his death. Ben only appears as a phantom
character, either in Willy's memories or, latterly, in private 'conversations' with his
younger brother and as an apparent symptom of Willy's delirium.

Ben represents the pioneering, adventuresome spirit of the beginning of the 20th
century when the American Dream was related to pitting oneself against the
elements and setting off for unknown regions in search of financial reward. Willy
is full of admiration for his brother who represents all that he wanted to become,
'The man knew what he wanted and went out and got it! Walked into a
jungle, and comes out, the age of twenty-one, and he's rich!' *(Act One)*.

Willy is uncritical of the means that Ben had to employ to become rich; indeed,
these are never specified. However, when Miller wrote the play, it was generally
understood that diamond mining was founded on the ruthless exploitation of the
indigenous African population and that the massive wealth yielded was not shared
with the native workforce. Ben as good as admits to employing unscrupulous
business tactics when he tricks Biff into a sparring match that ends up with Biff flat
on his back with the point of Ben's *'umbrella poised over'* his eye. *(Act One)*.

> **Key quotation**
>
> Never fight fair with a stranger, boy. You'll never get out of the jungle
> that way.
> *(Ben, Act One)*

As much as Willy admires Ben, he is swayed by Linda not to take up his offer to
manage Ben's timberland in Alaska. Linda uses Willy's own fantasies of future
success to persuade him that he is 'building something' with the firm and that,
like Dave Singleman, he will be able to make a living into his eighties *(Act Two)*. While
Linda perpetuates Willy's illusions by never questioning them, Ben is less credulous.

When Linda assures Willy that he is **'doing well enough'**, Ben quibbles, **'Enough for what, my dear?'** *(Act Two)*.

Later in the play, Willy appears to summon the spirit of his brother to ease his passing to the next world. He seeks his advice about killing himself to gain the insurance money for Biff. Ben is equivocal about it, at first warning Willy that he must avoid **'making a fool of'** himself *(Act Two)*. However, when he returns after Biff has wept in Willy's arms, Ben appears to have changed his mind, agreeing that Biff will be **'outstanding, with twenty thousand behind him'** *(Act Two)*.

Ben appears to equate the jungle with death in his last speeches. At the end of Act Two, he tells Willy that it is 'time' before moving off into the darkness and towards the **'The boat'**. Now, for the first time in the play, Ben refers to himself and Willy as 'we' as he acts as a conduit between life and death, warning Willy, **'We'll be late'**. Willy tries to follow him immediately, **'Ben! Ben, where do I...?** *[He makes a sudden movement of search]* **Ben, how do I ...?'** before rushing out into the night and suicide, the ultimate step into the unknown.

Activity 8

'Do you think Miller wants the audience to believe in Ben as an actual character or is he a product of Willy's capacity for myth-making?' Discuss this question in groups and find evidence for your point of view.

Ben is associated with the American Dream, with sibling rivalry, materialism and unscrupulousness. He functions as a 'tempter' figure to Willy, giving his seal of approval for Willy's suicidal plans. Ben also functions as a substitute father figure in psychoanalytical readings of the play.

Minor characters

Howard Wagner

Howard only appears once in the play and he is part of the action that takes place in the present. His function is to fire Willy from his job after over 30 years of service. Despite this, Miller has not demonized Howard but instead, through the device of the tape recorder, he presents him as a family man.

Although Howard flatly refuses to find a spot for Willy in New York, his decisions appear to be based on sound business principles and he is reasonably patient with Willy, despite Willy's patronizing and hectoring behaviour. Nevertheless, Howard represents the face of capitalism that puts profit before loyalty.

Howard speaks casually and insensitively about the expensive hobbies that he is able to pursue and of his latest acquisition, the wire recorder, which cost a, not insubstantial, $150. By implication, he discards Willy like orange peel and does not honour any of the promises that Willy claims, accurately or not, that he was made by Howard's father.

Howard is not a fully developed character. His function, through firing Willy, is to act as a catalyst to Willy's state of desperation and eventual suicide. Howard is associated with the themes of family relationships, the American Dream, capitalism and wealth. He acts as a foil to Charley, who is a more benevolent capitalist, and may perhaps be compared to Ben in his more ruthless attitude towards 'survival'.

> **Activity 9**
>
> Re-read the scene in Howard's office and make notes about its function in the play. Think about how it contributes to our understanding of themes and characters, and how it contributes to the progress of the drama.

The Woman

The Woman is not given a name in the cast list by Miller. This may be because the character represents a succession of similar types of women that Willy may have had affairs with during his 30 years on the road. Alternatively, her lack of a name and the use of the definite article could imply that the Woman is Willy's only indiscretion and that by identifying her simply as the Woman, Miller is signalling the destructive impact her discovery had on Willy's relationship with Biff.

In either case, Willy's memories of the Woman are guilty ones. In the first memory, which is anticipated by the sound of the Woman's laughter, Willy remembers himself in a favourable light. The Woman thinks that he is 'a wonderful man' *(Act One)*. She appreciates his joking as well as his generosity with the stockings.

The Woman's second manifestation in Willy's memory is less comfortable, culminating as it does with her being bundled, half-dressed, into the hall. Indeed, Willy could be accused of treating the Woman like the 'piece of fruit' he complains to Howard about *(Act Two)*. When Biff turns up unexpectedly, Willy acts disrespectfully towards the Woman, in front of his son, telling lies about who she is and humiliating her.

The Woman functions as a physical manifestation of Willy's guilt, both towards Linda and towards Biff. She is associated with themes related to the role of women in society as well as to loneliness. In a feminist reading of the play she is the whore figure to Linda's perfect wife.

The Woman is a physical manifestation of Willy's guilt; Brian Dennehy plays Willy and Abigail McKern plays the Woman in the 2005 production at the Lyric Theatre, London

Miss Forsythe and Letta

Although very minor characters, the two women that Happy picks up demonstrate both his sexual magnetism and their mutual willingness to indulge in meaningless relationships. The two young women are associated with themes of lies and deceit, the role of women, and sexual conquest. Like the Woman, both Miss Forsythe and Letta are seen as objects, and Happy's decision to abandon his father for an evening of pleasure with these new acquaintances reflect especially badly on his character. They also highlight the 'sale of self' idea that relates both to Willy and to the Woman.

Activity 10

Write a plan for an essay about Miller's presentation of women in this play. Do you see it as misogynistic in any way? Consider the pros and cons in your plan.

Writing about characters

You may be asked to write about one or more characters and to consider either how Miller presents each character or how he uses individual characters to communicate his ideas to an audience.

Aim to refer to the following, where applicable:

- the appearance of the character, if stated, and what they sound like
- what the character says about themselves and about others
- what other characters say about them
- how the character interacts with other characters
- comparisons and/or contrasts with other characters
- what the character does, their actions and reactions to events
- the type of language the character uses.

When thinking about the purpose or function of the character, you should consider whether they:

- give information about off-stage events or events that occurred before the time-frame of the play
- develop the plot
- act as a catalyst to bring a change of direction to the story
- act as a foil or contrast to other characters
- contribute to major themes of the play
- alter the mood or atmosphere, e.g. creating comedy or pathos.

All plays are written to be performed on a stage in front of a live audience. The language of the play is just one of a series of elements, including movement, facial expressions, set and costume, that the audience experience and create meaning from.

As readers of modern plays, we are aware of an additional aspect of language in the text: the stage directions.

Stage directions

The stage directions express the playwright's intentions for how the play is presented to an audience. Stage directions frequently include indications of setting, atmosphere or the appearance of the characters in a scene.

However, not all stage directions are purely functional. Miller's directions in this play, especially in the opening sequence, are often expressed poetically and the **figurative language** that he uses deserves close attention.

The first stage directions of *Death of a Salesman*, for Act One, begin with a reference to the atmospheric flute music that opens the play. The description of the melody, *'small and fine, telling of grass and trees and the horizon'* is a particularly impressionistic direction indicating that the music should suggest an idyllic, outdoor setting, with the word 'horizon' conjuring up images of extensive space. To a *reader* of the play, the impressionistic language used here creates the atmosphere, which, in the theatre, would be created through the melody itself.

Miller then suggests the closing in upon this idealized setting, in the next line of quite abstract directions: *Before us is the Salesman's house. We are aware of towering, angular shapes behind it, surrounding it on all sides.* This description is a substitute, for the reader, for what the set and lighting designers will achieve for an audience in the theatre. By using the plural personal pronoun 'we' here, Miller invites the reader to become a part of the 'virtual' audience and to imagine the *'towering angular shapes'*, which appear to be both intimidating yet not fully defined.

Indeed, Miller stresses the **impressionistic** nature of aspects of the setting by using figurative language, **personifying** one aspect of the lighting state (the colour, angle and/or intensity of the stage lanterns used at any one time in a production) with *'the surrounding area shows an angry glow of orange'*, and personifying another as by describing how *'An air of the dream clings to the place, a dream rising out of reality'* (Act One).

---

figurative language language that uses figures of speech, is metaphorical and not literal

impressionistic language that creates personal ideas and impressions rather than literal facts

personification a device whereby a writer assigns qualities of a living person to inanimate objects

---

Lighting and background images help to create the atmosphere of the Loman home in the Royal Shakespeare Company's production in 2015, with Sam Marks as Happy and Alex Hassel as Biff

After a fairly literal and lengthy description of the configuration of the set and its furnishings, Miller uses more figurative language in his description of Willy's nature and of Linda's attitude towards her husband. Miller uses metaphor to describe Linda as having developed *'an iron repression of her exceptions to Willy's behaviour'* (Act One). He describes Willy's nature as *'mercurial'*, alluding to the Roman god Mercury, who was famous for his multiple and changeable character traits. Mercury's status as god of 'salesmen' is probably intended to allude to Willy's occupation as well as to his nature. Miller also uses **antonyms** to compare Willy's *'massive'* dreams with his *'little cruelties'*; he uses vivid metaphors to describe Linda's *'sharp reminders'* of Willy's *'turbulent longings'*. Each of these adjectives suggests discomfort or disturbance, and helps to prepare the reader for some of the discord that features in the play.

antonym a word that has the opposite meaning to another word, e.g. 'big', 'little'

Later in the play, the stage directions are more factual and functional, although they are vital in indicating the shifts between the scenes set in 'real time' and those set in Willy's memories or imagination. Some of these refer to actors crossing the wall-line on stage to show that real time has dissolved, as when Ben greets Willy in Act One, **'So you're William'** and the stage direction reads, *'As Willy comes towards him through the wall-line of the kitchen'*.

However, there are still examples, throughout the play, where the directions are suggestive rather than explicit. When Willy is planting his seeds in Act Two, Miller describes him as being *'in the blue of night'* and, just before he leaves the stage for the last time, Miller's directions describe Willy as *'elegiacally, turning to the house'*, which suggests that Willy has somehow become an embodiment of a song mourning someone's death at a funeral.

> ### Activity 1
>
> Read the stage directions from Act One, *'Light has risen on the boys' room...'* to *'...hard-skinned, although seemingly more content'*. They act as an introduction to the characters of Biff and Happy.
>
> **a)** Annotate these stage directions to indicate which will help the director and actors to interpret the roles and which are intended to inform a reader of the boys' individual characters.
>
> **b)** Highlight any figurative language in the directions and explain its effect.

Dramatic language – characters' dialogue

The dramatic language that Miller employs in *Death of a Salesman* is crafted to sound something like the **vernacular speech** of Brooklyn, New York, in the middle of the 20th century. This speech is often referred to as Brooklynese because of the distinctive use of dialect and language characteristic of residents of Brooklyn.

Miller's dialogue echoes the way that family members interact with one another as well as with other characters they are familiar with. To make the dialogue more natural sounding, he also includes the informalities, repetitions and hesitations, within the speeches, that mimic the way we communicate with people we know well; this is an aspect of the genre of realism, contributing to the creation of an authentic setting and **social milieu** on stage.

> **social milieu** the physical environment and social class of the characters who inhabit it
>
> **vernacular speech** a language or dialect that is native to a particular region or country rather than to a literary or cultured language

Features of spoken language

Some of the features of spoken language that Miller employs to create authentic-sounding conversation include the use of pauses and repetition, **backchannels**, conjunctions, present historic tense, and **sociolect**.

Use of pause, hesitation, repetition and non-sequitur

Conversational language is spontaneously constructed and therefore less fluent than written language. Most playwrights cut away the redundant phrases and false starts that punctuate real-life conversation, but, to simulate natural speech, Miller includes some of the hesitations, repetitions, pauses and **non-sequiturs** that are typical of everyday interactions. For example, when Willy encounters Bernard in Charley's office, he finds the contrast between Bernard's success and Biff's 'failure' too uncomfortable to process and this is reflected in his disjointed reply to Bernard, which is marked by pauses and dashes as he struggles to continue the conversation.

Key quotation

BERNARD: You still with the old firm, Willy?

WILLY [*after a pause*]: I'm – I'm overjoyed to see how you made the grade, Bernard, overjoyed. It's an encouraging thing to see a young man really – really – Looks very good for Biff – very – [*He breaks off, then*] Bernard – [*He is so full of emotion, he breaks off again.*] (*Act Two*)

backchannel little words or sounds made in conversation that do not interrupt the speaker but acknowledge that the listener is listening

lexis the linguistic term for words, terms, expression

non-sequitur a statement (or a response) that does not follow logically from or is not clearly related to anything previously said

semantic field a group of words connected by a shared field of reference, e.g. words associated with light and darkness or with nature

semantics in linguistics, refers to the study of meaning

sociolect a language style associated with a particular social group; the 'style' includes use of grammatical construction, choice of **lexis** and deployment of **semantic fields**

Activity 2

a) What effect do you think Miller intends to create through the linguistic devices of pause, dashes and non-sequitur in the example above?

b) Find other examples from the play where Miller presents a character struggling to complete what they are saying and write a sentence or two about the effects created in each case.

Use of backchannels

Listeners may respond to the speaker by saying 'mmm' or using little words like 'yeah', which do not interrupt the speaker but acknowledge that they are listening. These are called backchannels, or minimal responses. For example, Happy punctuates Linda's description of Willy's state of mind with such empty, non-committal responses.

> **Key quotation**
>
> LINDA: No, a lot of people think he's lost his – balance. But you don't have to be very smart to know what his trouble is. The man is exhausted.
>
> HAPPY: Sure!
>
> LINDA: A small man can be just as exhausted as a great man.
> *(Act One)*

Frequent use of conjunctions

When people are speaking, they do not have the time to think about varying the way they present a narrative or to select the most appropriate conjunction for joining their ideas together. The most frequently used conjunction is 'and'. However, in discussion (interactional discourse), preferred conjunctions are often 'so' and 'but'. 'So' implies that what follows is a logical extension of what went before, whereas 'but' indicates opposition. For example, when Willy confronts Howard about finding him a job in New York, both men frequently employ the word 'but' as a way of registering their opposition to one another.

> **Key quotation**
>
> HOWARD: Oh, I could understand that, Willy. But you're a road man, Willy, and we do a road business. We've only got a half-dozen salesmen on the floor here.
>
> WILLY: God knows, Howard, I never asked a favour of any man. But I was with the firm when your father used to carry you in here in his arms.
>
> HOWARD: I know that, Willy, but –
>
> WILLY: Your father came to me the day you were born and asked me what I thought of the name of Howard, may he rest in peace.
>
> HOWARD: I appreciate that, Willy, but there just is no spot here for you.
> *(Act One)*

Use of historic present tense

When a present tense verb refers to a past event, the tense is termed the conversational historical present. People often use this in their speech to make their description of the past appear more immediate. For example, when Linda describes what has happened to Willy at work she uses this spoken convention to emphasize the injustice of what has happened to him.

> **Key quotation**
>
> He <u>works</u> for a company thirty-six years this March, <u>opens up</u> unheard-of territories to their trademark, and now in his old age they take his salary away.
> *(Linda, Act One)*

Use of the sociolect of lower middle-class inhabitants of Brooklyn

Although class stratification has always been less clear cut in America than in Britain, it is possible to identify the characters in this play as belonging to a lower middle-class group (home owners, stay-at-home wife, 'white-collar' working husband, ownership of labour-saving appliances and leisure goods) and their speech is constructed to reflect that sociolect. For example, when Biff and Happy are talking, they use a mixture of:

- standard grammatical constructions
- non-standard grammatical constructions
- abbreviated word forms
- slang
- cliché.

> **Key quotation**
>
> HAPPY [*looking toward where Linda went out*]: What a woman! They broke the mould when they made her. You know that, Biff? [...]
>
> HAPPY: Well, let's face it: he's no hot-shot selling man. Except that sometimes, you have to admit, he's a sweet personality.
>
> BIFF [*deciding*]: Lend me ten bucks, will ya? I want to buy some new ties.
>
> HAPPY: I'll take you to a place I know. Beautiful stuff. Wear one of my striped shirts tomorrow.
>
> BIFF: She got grey. Mom got awful old. Gee. I'm gonna go in to Oliver tomorrow and knock him for a –
>
> HAPPY: Come on up. Tell that to Dad. Let's give him a whirl. Come on.
>
> BIFF [*steamed up*]: You know, with ten thousand bucks, boy!
> *(Act One)*

Activity 3

a) Identify in the dialogue above where each of the features of the sociolect appear.

b) Explain, in a paragraph, what effects Miller creates through this exchange.

Language and characterization

All of the Loman family, with the exception of Ben, use similar language, reflecting their shared history and social background. Charley also mainly converses in the informal register of their sociolect. Although Charley is a successful businessman, the impression that Miller gives is that he is self-made, not highly educated, and that he is from ordinary stock. His speaks in a similar way to Willy.

> **Key quotation**
>
> **WILLY** [*as Charley takes out his wallet*]: The Supreme Court! And he didn't even mention it!
>
> **CHARLEY** [*counting out money on the desk*]: He don't have to – he's gonna do it.
>
> **WILLY:** And you never told him what to do, did you? You never took any interest in him.
>
> **CHARLEY:** My salvation is that I never took any interest in anything. There's some money – fifty dollars. I got an accountant inside.
>
> **WILLY:** Charley, look... [*With difficulty*] I got my insurance to pay. If you can manage it – I need a hundred and ten dollars.
> (Act Two)

Both characters use the non-standard grammatical construction 'I got' rather than 'I have'. Charley says 'he don't' rather than 'he doesn't'. He also uses the elided form 'he's gonna' rather than 'he is going to' – a form used by all of the characters in the play, apart from Ben, at one time or another.

Although Bernard is a slightly 'bookish' character, his language is not significantly distinguishable from that of the Loman boys, apart from the lack of coarseness in his vocabulary and a tendency to use more formal grammatical constructions.

It is possible to notice a slight difference between the way that all the younger characters speak when they are appearing as teenagers in Willy's memory and the way they speak as adults in the episodes that take place in Willy's real time. For example, when Biff and Happy are presented as teenagers, **exclamations** such as 'Gee' and 'Boy!' appear more frequently in their speech than when they are presented as adults, as Miller uses these to indicate their lack of maturity. When they are adults, their exclamations are closer to swearing.

exclamation a word used to express surprise or shock or a strong emotion about something; the type of phrase or clause associated with exclamations is called exclamative

God Almighty, Mom, how
long has he been doing this?
(Biff, Act One)

Those ungrateful bastards!
(Biff, Act One)

Willy

Although Willy's speech is consistent
with the established sociolect in
the play, Miller gives him some
distinguishing linguistic features.
In particular, Willy is prone to
contradiction. Miller makes the
audience aware of this linguistic
characteristic in the opening minutes
of the play when he first describes
Biff as 'a lazy bum!' before insisting,
'There's one thing about Biff –
he's not lazy' *(Act One)*.

The second feature specific to
Willy is his repetition of a series of
hackneyed platitudes, which he
uses to support and to justify the
guiding principles of his life.

In his memories, Willy talks about driving the
red Chevrolet; Dustin Hoffman as Willy in the
1985 TV film

...the man who makes an appearance in the business world, the man
who creates personal interest, is the man who gets ahead. Be liked and
you will never want.
(Willy, Act One)

...it's not what you do, Ben. It's who you know and the smile on your
face! It's contacts, Ben, contacts!
(Willy, Act Two)

These precepts are spoken with such passion and with such belief in their universal
truth that they reassure Willy that he has not wasted his life while simultaneously
preventing him from recognizing their essential emptiness.

hackneyed platitude an expression such as a cliché, which is unimaginative and
commonplace

Ben

Ben has a slightly different way of expressing himself from the other characters in the play. Miller presents him as quite a formal character with a limited range of expression. His speech is more stilted than the living characters and he is the only character to address Willy, formally, as 'William'.

Given that the phantom Ben is a manifestation of Willy's fevered imagination; that his acquaintance with Willy, when he was alive, was brief and sporadic; that he did not settle in Brooklyn; and that he is, in any case, dead, it is unsurprising that he does not talk like the other Lomans or, indeed, like the other characters in the play.

Key quotations

At that age I had a very faulty view of geography, William. I discovered after a few days that I was heading due south, so instead of Alaska, I ended up in Africa.
(Ben, Act One)

William, you're being first-rate with your boys. Outstanding, manly chaps!
(Ben, Act One)

Ben's use of language is closer to Standard English than any other character's in the play and it may have been Miller's intention to show how his extensive travel and experience in the colonies has resulted in a more anglicized form of speech.

Ben is always in a hurry and always appears to have somewhere that he would rather be than with his little brother Willy. This may account for the brevity of his utterances. He is also a cynical commentator on Willy's job and his dreams for the future; he is unimpressed with Willy's career of **'Selling'**, backchannelling without commitment to reveal a lack of interest, uttering a scathing, **'Yes. Well...'** *(Act One)*; and is equally underwhelmed by Willy's mention of hunting in Brooklyn, merely responding with a bland, **'Really, now'** *(Act One)*. When Willy excitedly outlines his future with the firm and his ambitions to be like Dave Singleman, Ben lets out a cynical, **'Bah!'** *(Act Two)*.

The twin themes of Ben's speeches relate to the opportunities to be had in other continents, specifically in the jungle of Africa and the timberlands of Alaska, and to acquiring wealth.

He also frequently refers to the time, looks at his watch and mentions his mode of transport to his next appointment; the fact that he gave Willy a watch fob with a diamond in it links him securely, both linguistically and metaphorically, with the theme of time.

The following quotations reveal Miller's use of the semantic fields of time, place and methods of transportation.

Key quotations

I only have a few minutes.
(Ben, Act One)

[*glancing at his watch*]: I have an appointment in Ketchikan Tuesday week.
(Ben, Act One)

I'll be late for my train.
(Ben, Act One)

Activity 4

Go back through Ben's several appearances and choose two sequences of interaction between him and Willy.

a) Compare the two brothers' speech patterns, specifically looking at:

- the number and type of questions that Willy asks Ben

- how Ben replies to these questions

- the semantic fields used by Ben that help to identify him as a man-of-action.

b) Explain how Miller presents the characters of Ben and Willy through speech.

Figurative language, motifs, symbols and images

Although some commentators maintain that Miller's use of language is unpoetic, there are many instances in the play where Miller uses figurative language, repeated images or **symbols** to help to convey an additional layer of meaning to the audience or where the characters speak more lyrically than the sociolect might suggest. This is one of the features of Miller's writing that supports the tragic style of this play.

Language, imagery and symbolism associated with time and memory

As *Death of a Salesman* is a memory play, one of its key themes is time and, therefore, one of the most frequently repeated references or **motifs** in the play relates to the passage of time and to the past as well as to the future.

motif a word, phrase, image, idea or sound used in literature that is repeated and builds up a resonance through its repeated patterning; in *Death of a Salesman*, motifs include references to time, repeated phrases such as being well liked, references to the woods, forests, or the jungle, to the silk stockings, etc.

symbol an object that represents or extends deeper implications about character or situation than may be suggested by their surface appearance

Words that relate to time appear on over 50 different occasions in a play that covers a relatively short time period – the last 24 hours of Willy Loman's life.

> **Key quotations**
>
> When you write you're coming, he's all smiles, and talks about the future, and – he's just wonderful. And then the closer you seem to come, the more shaky he gets, and then, by the time you get here, he's arguing, and he seems angry at you.
> *(Linda, Act One)*
>
> Figure it out. Work a lifetime to pay off a house. You finally own it, and there's nobody to live in it.
> *(Willy, Act One)*

> **Activity 5**
>
> Look for examples of vocabulary related specifically to time and to the past or the future, and make some notes relating to Miller's use of this semantic field of time in preparation for writing an assessment piece on Miller's use of figurative language in the play.

The language of nature: gardens, trees and jungles

Another very significant use of figurative or repeated language relates to nature – to gardens, flowers, plants and trees, as well as to forests, timberlands and jungle. Miller creates an **antithesis** between domestic nature found in man-made gardens, the planting of seeds and the growing of vegetables for the family to eat and wild nature represented by the 'grand outdoors' *(Act Two)*, the wide open spaces of America and the new continents beyond.

> **antithesis** a direct opposite or contrast

Willy longs for the semi-rural setting of the house that Linda and he bought when the children were small. He resents the loss of his prized elm trees and of the light that used to flood the house and garden and nourish the plants. In Act One, he complains that, 'The grass don't grow any more, you can't raise a carrot in the back yard'. Willy's rhapsody about his lost garden is one of his most lyrical moments in the play.

More and more I think of those days, Linda. This time of year it was lilac and wisteria. And then the peonies would come out, and the daffodils. What a fragrance in this room!
(Willy, Act One)

Miller contrasts this image of tranquillity and fragrance with the rugged beauty of the wild outdoors. Uncultivated America is imagined in Ben's description of the semi-mythical character of Willy's **'wild-hearted'** father, driving his team **'right across the country'** in his **'wagon'** before embarking for the challenges of the harsh terrain of Alaska *(Act One)*.

While Willy struggles to overcome the natural limitations of his shady garden, Ben has travelled to both Africa and Alaska and struck it rich in each of these contrasting but heavily-wooded terrains. Ben experiences the extremes of nature in the jungles of Africa and the timberlands of Alaska while Willy enjoys the more modest **'two beautiful elm trees'** in his garden *(Act One)*. For Willy, in his memories in Act One,

Willy yearns for the lost Eden of his original garden; a publicity still for the 1985 TV production

his happiness was to be found **'swingin' there under those branches'** of the two elms not forging a future or chasing a fortune in distant continents. Perhaps Miller intends us to draw comparisons between Willy's cultivated flowers and Ben's wild ones, supporting the contrast between the two brothers and their different interpretations of the American Dream, as well as sowing the metaphorical seeds of Willy's love of nature.

After his vivid and disturbing memory of Biff's discovery of the existence of the Woman, Willy is suddenly impelled to buy seeds on his way home from the restaurant. The seeds need to be seen as the symbols they are, representing for Willy possibilities of a future. In a state of high agitation, Willy asks Stanley the waiter, **'is there a seed store'**, telling him desperately, **'Nothing's planted. I don't have a thing in the ground'** *(Act Two)*, which appears to equate to his sense of having nothing to pass on to the next generation, primarily to Biff.

Activity 6

While Willy appears to appreciate nature for its intrinsic beauty, Ben chooses to exploit it for personal gain. Find evidence for this viewpoint in the language that each character uses about nature.

Use of metaphor and irony: fire

Willy twice uses metaphorical language related to burning woodland to describe the impending crisis that impels him to suicide. Having initially told Linda about his literal journey to Yonkers, when he marvelled at the beauty of the scenery and the thickness of the trees, Willy snaps at Happy's consoling offer to **'retire you for life'**, shouting, **'Where are you guys, where are you? The woods are burning!'** *(Act One)* The metaphor clearly refers to the speed of destruction caused by a forest fire, its resistance to being extinguished and its power to engulf everything in its path. In Act Two, Willy repeats this metaphor, linking the image of the burning woods with the ironic image of the blaze caused by his being 'fired' by Howard.

> **Key quotation**
>
> **I'm not interested in stories about the past or any crap of that kind because the woods are burning, boys, you understand? There's a big blaze going on all around. I was fired today.**
> *(Willy, Act Two)*

Miller also names Mr Birnbaum, the teacher who flunked Biff at maths. The name is a compound of 'birn' (pronounced 'burn') and 'baum', which is the German name for 'tree'. It is no coincidence that Mr Birnbaum's decision to fail Biff ignited the rift between Biff and his father as it sends Biff to Boston seeking help from his father only to discover disillusionment in the guise of the Woman.

Fire also features in the aftermath of Biff's discovery when, according to Bernard, Biff returned from Boston and took the sneakers that he was so proud of, that he had printed with the legend 'the University of Virginia' **'down in the cellar, and burned them up in the furnace'** *(Act Two)*.

Later, completing the series of fire images, Biff begs Willy to burn his dream:

> **Key quotation**
>
> **BIFF** [*crying, broken*]**: Will you let me go, for Christ's sake? Will you take that phony dream and burn it before something happens?** [*Struggling to contain himself, he pulls away and moves to the stairs.*] **I'll go in the morning.**
> *(Act Two)*

Activity 7

Burning is the most irrevocable method of destruction. Write a paragraph to explain how Miller's references to fire are linked and what their cumulative effect is.

Classical allusions and hyperbole

Other figurative language such as **classical allusions** and **hyperbole** may be found in Willy's descriptions of his boys when they were teenagers.

Willy uses two classical allusions to magnify the potential achievement of his sons. Having dismissed Bernard as a **'pest'** and **'an anaemic'** *(Act One)*, Willy compares his own boys to heroes from Greek myth. He compares them both to Adonis, singling out Biff to be likened to **'a young god'**, which he then revises to Hercules *(Act One)*. By imagining the boys to be cast in the mould of these two legendary figures, Willy convinces his sons, as well as himself, that they are above ordinary boys and men. This leads to a situation where both Linda and Willy are less complimentary about their grown-up sons, who have turned out to be such disappointments compared to Willy's wild ambitions for them.

> **classical allusion** figurative language that compares events or characters from the classical world of myth to modern parallels
>
> **hyperbole** a form of overstatement or exaggeration

Hercules and Adonis

Hercules is the Roman name for the Greek demi-god Heracles, the son of the god Zeus and the mortal woman Alcmene. Hercules is famed for his massive physical strength and endurance and his adventures throughout the ancient Greek world.

In Greek mythology, Adonis was the god of beauty and desire beloved by Aphrodite, the goddess of love.

> **Key quotations**
>
> That's why I thank Almighty God you're both built like Adonises.
> *(Willy, Act One)*
>
> Like a young god. Hercules – something like that. And the sun, the sun all around him.
> *(Willy, Act One)*
>
> Biff is a lazy bum!
> *(Willy, Act One)*
>
> You louse. You...
> *(Linda, Act Two)*

The terms in the last two quotations above appear to be even more derogatory in the light of Willy's earlier hyperbolic praise.

Symbolic language and concrete visual symbols

Miller uses a number of symbols in the play that are either seen or referred to, and which carry meaning over and above their superficial appearances.

Diamonds are referred to both literally and figuratively. The diamond watch fob and Ben's own watch are both real items and symbolic ones. While Ben made his fortune in real diamond mines and literally gave Willy a watch fob with a diamond in it, in the closing moments of the play the diamond comes to represent Willy's legacy for Biff, to be achieved through Willy's death. Willy has already literally pawned the diamond-studded watch fob to pay for one of Biff's courses that led him nowhere; now he is pawning the 'diamond' of his life to rescue Biff's future.

> **Key quotations**
>
> WILLY: Whatever happened to that diamond watch fob? Remember? When Ben came from Africa that time? Didn't he give me a watch fob with a diamond in it?
>
> LINDA: You pawned it, dear. Twelve, thirteen years ago. For Biff's radio correspondence course.
> *(Act One)*
>
> WILLY [*now assured, with rising power*]: Oh, Ben, that's the whole beauty of it! I see it like a diamond, shining in the dark, hard and rough, that I can pick up and touch in my hand.
> *(Willy, Act Two)*

Activity 8

Think about the symbolic value of some other objects that appear in the play, as listed below.

- silk stockings
- Ben's valise and umbrella
- Bill Oliver's pen
- Bernard's tennis racquet
- Biff's sneakers with their printed logo
- Champagne and lobsters
- wire recorder
- Willy's sample cases
- seed packets and seeds
- Linda's basket of washing

Writing about language

Whatever type of question you answer, ensure that you demonstrate your understanding of the way Miller uses language and in particular:

- the approximation of everyday speech in Brooklyn in the 1940s, including:
  - sociolect
  - repetition and non-sequitur
  - hesitation, pause and ellipses
  - choice of lexis and use of semantic fields
  - slang, cliché, swearing and exclamatives
- figurative speech, imagery, symbol and metaphor
- allusion, hyperbole
- the less natural speech pattern of Ben, the dead brother.

Dreams

The American Dream is embedded deep in the American psyche and is a central theme in *Death of a Salesman*. We have already looked at the two mainstream versions of the American Dream: the conquering of the great outdoors, acquiring land and a livelihood (or fortune); and working hard within society to gain wealth and to pass that wealth on to the next generation.

Through Willy Loman, Miller explores a particular manifestation of the American Dream. Willy has a huge capacity to dream and he believes that through his work as a salesman, he can gain status, respect and

The American Dream in the 1950s included a beautiful home on one's own plot of land and the latest car model

wealth for his family. Throughout the play, he rebuilds his dreams and refuses to accept that he can't provide a great future, even though this eventually requires his own death.

Willy's dream is founded on the idea that material success is granted to those who are 'well-liked' and who have 'personal attractiveness' *(Act One)*. He disparages Bernard, who does not match these criteria, and then is surprised when Bernard confounds his prediction by outstripping Biff and Hap's achievements.

Willy confuses the pleasures to be derived from material possessions with the contentment that comes from personal happiness and a loving family. Although Willy is described as being 'wonderful with his hands' and 'a happy man with a batch of cement' *(Requiem)*, and though he decries the manhood of any male who 'can't handle tools' *(Act One)*, he puts his energy into selling, which he sees as a better class of occupation, and he feels his dreams are thwarted because Biff makes his living doing manual jobs. This is why Biff laments at his graveside that 'He had the wrong dreams. All, all, wrong' *(Requiem)*.

While Biff does finally recognize the worthlessness of Willy's dreams, Hap has accepted Willy's distorted version. Hap lives by his father's tired cliché's about being 'well-liked' and valuing the business world of 'selling or buying' that Biff has dismissed as a 'measly manner of existence' *(Act One)*.

Nevertheless, Miller leaves it to Charley to deliver a final judgement on Willy's dreams and he is remarkably forgiving of his neighbour, who has exploited his good nature for years: 'Nobody dast blame this man [...] A salesman is got to dream, boy. It comes with the territory' *(Requiem)*.

Write a plan, then an introductory paragraph for this essay question:

'He had the wrong dreams. All, all, wrong.' How far do you agree that Willy's tragedy resulted from his having the wrong dreams?

Truth and lies; illusions, delusions and secrets

Willy lies to Linda, he lies to his sons and he lies to himself.

> **Key quotation**
>
> **Oh, I'll knock 'em dead next week. I'll go to Hartford. I'm very well liked in Hartford. You know, the trouble is, Linda, people don't seem to take to me.**
> *(Willy, Act One)*

In this brief speech Miller shows us Willy's essentially contradictory nature, his boundless facility for self-deception, which suddenly (and uncharacteristically) falls away to recognition of the truth.

Throughout the play, Willy is in denial about the cause of his fractured relationship with Biff, the exposure of his secret affair with the Woman in Boston. The way in which he has suppressed this truth can be seen as a source of the psychosis that causes him to experience moments from his past in such a vivid way and to hallucinate about his recently dead brother.

The theme of truth and lies is related to Willy's dreams as it is only in the fictional world that his mind creates that he can tell Linda that he has earned **'roughly two hundred gross'** on his trip to Providence and Boston, when in reality he has earned **'seventy dollars and some pennies'** *(Act One)*. More importantly, in his dreams, he is good at his job, popular with the buyers and well-liked by all in his business life, with two **'outstanding, manly chaps'** for sons at home.

In reality, Willy has always struggled to meet the household bills and is in a state of perpetual fear that he won't **'make a living for you, or a business, a business for the boys'** *(Act One)*.

Willy's illusions have been perpetuated through the acquiescence of Linda, who appears to have refused to exercise any kind of check upon his capacity for myth-making. She flatters his ego and is complicit in his misrepresentation of himself. She calls him the **'handsomest man in the world'**, **'lively'** rather than overly talkative, and tells him he is **'doing wonderful'** *(Act One)*, even when he clearly isn't. Some commentators blame Linda for failing to rein in Willy's delusional views.

This failure is symbolized in the play by her cowardice in relation to the rubber tube that she has found. While accepting that Willy is feeling suicidal, Linda fails to confront him about it. For fear of insulting her husband, Linda's lack of intervention leads directly to his death.

> **Key quotation**
>
> I'm – I'm ashamed to. How can I mention it to him? Every day I go down and take away that little rubber pipe. But, when he comes home, I put it back where it was. How can I insult him that way? I don't know what to do.
> *(Linda, Act Two)*

According to Willy's memories, his boys idolized him when they were growing up, an idea that is corroborated by Linda. However, this corroboration is also a part of Willy's memory and cannot be taken at face value.

In the 'real time' scenes, there is little evidence of the boys understanding their father and, although Happy continually strives for Willy's good opinion, his treatment of him in the restaurant reveals a callous disregard for his well-being. By following in his father's footsteps as a salesman, and by emulating Willy's ambitions for material success, Happy lends credence to Willy's fundamental philosophy of life.

Only Biff has the courage to challenge Willy's delusions about himself. Biff is unable to forgive Will's betrayal of Linda and, although Willy assured him, **'when you grow up you'll understand about these things'**, when Willy's secret affair was revealed *(Act Two)*, Biff did not understand. Biff's rejection of his father, based on his new perception of him as a **'fake'** *(Act One)*, had the potential power to save Willy from himself. However, Miller shows that by retreating into his illusory world where his status as successful 'paterfamilias' is unchallenged, Willy remains on his headlong plunge towards personal tragedy and death.

Biff tries one more time, after the Bill Oliver fiasco, to reach his father, to shake hands with him and to make peace and, when that fails, he is forced to confront Willy with the truth about himself. The 'discovery' of the rubber tube, which Willy refuses to admit he knows anything about, is the catalyst to Biff's exposure of all the lies that underpin the Loman household.

> **Key quotation**
>
> BIFF [*to Happy*]: The man don't know who we are! The man is gonna know! [*To Willy*] We never told the truth for ten minutes in this house!
> *(Act Two)*

Activity 2

a) Go through the play and make a list of all the lies that are told. Remember to include self-deception and flattery.

b) How far do you agree with Biff's assertion, in the closing section of Act Two, that Willy **'don't know who we are'**? Plan your response, exploring the sections of the play where Willy is not on stage to support your answer. Consider sections where Biff and Happy are alone together discussing Willy and where Linda speaks to her sons about their father's decline.

Memories, nostalgia and change

As a memory play, the substance of the action is punctuated with Willy's memories and Miller supports this with numerous repeated references to remembering. In fact, the word 'remember' appears nearly 50 times in the course of the short play.

> **Key quotations**
>
> **My God! Remember how they used to follow him around in high school? When he smiled at one of them their faces lit up. When he walked down the street...** [*He loses himself in reminiscences.*]
> *(Willy, Act One)*
>
> **Remember that big Betsy something – what the hell was her name – over on Bushwick Avenue?**
> *(Biff, Act One)*
>
> **Spite, spite, is the word of your undoing! And when you're down and out, remember what did it. When you're rotting somewhere beside the railroad tracks, remember, and don't you dare blame it on me!**
> *(Willy, Act Two)*

Willy looks back to his barely remembered childhood, sitting under a wagon in South Dakota. He asks Ben to **'tell about Dad'**, wanting to be able to tell his boys **'the kind of stock they spring from'** *(Act One)*. Without a father in his life, Willy has always felt **'kind of temporary'** *(Act One)* about himself and in his own family he has tried to 'put down roots' metaphorically and literally by buying a house away from the city and by planting a garden. Over the years, Willy's idyllic home has been eroded by 'progress' and he complains about the street being **'lined with cars'** *(Act One)*. Willy's garden has been **'massacred'** by the cutting down of the elm trees; his wisteria and peonies no longer grow in the shade of the neighbouring apartment buildings and even the grass won't grow any more *(Act One)*. This information comes right at the beginning of the play, showing that Miller is keen to establish Willy's nostalgia for the past and a sense of 'paradise' lost.

Ironically, though Willy is a salesman, he appears to despise and resist the advances of technology. He is frustrated by the unreliability of the consumer goods that he is still paying for, like the faulty refrigerator and his Chevrolet with its wayward steering. In Howard's office, when he confronts a machine that can replicate the past exactly, unlike his own self-flattering memory and unreliable perceptions, Willy suffers a mini-breakdown, crying out for Howard and begging him to 'Shut it off! Shut It off!' *(Act Two).*

Activity 3

Willy's resistance to change is shown in a number of different ways throughout the play, starting with the apparently trivial refusal to try the whipped cheese that Linda has bought for him, as a change and a surprise.

Find other examples of Willy's fixed mind-set and how this may have contributed to his breakdown.

Fathers, sons and sibling rivalry

Closely connected to the American Dream is another of Miller's themes: the relationship between fathers and sons. The aspiration at the heart of the American Dream falls on the father, who is patriarch and provider for the family. As the father ages, he invests his dreams for the future in the success of his sons.

Fathers and sons

Miller invites the audience to compare several father–son relationships in *Death of a Salesman.* Willy's relationship with Biff and Happy is central, but we are also asked compare this with the relationship between Charley and his son Bernard, as well as with Willy and his own absent father.

The whole crisis of the play is set in motion by the return of the prodigal Biff after a long absence. We learn that as soon as Biff 'got off the train' *(Act One),* Willy was criticizing him for not making any money, for not living up to his expectations of him.

Biff's return triggers conflict between father and son; from the 1985 TV adaptation with Dustin Hoffman as Willy and John Malkovich as Biff

Later, Biff blames his father for never having 'got anywhere because you blew me so full of hot air I could never stand taking orders from anybody! That's whose fault it is!' *(Act Two)*. The play corroborates Biff's accusation, showing Willy turning a blind eye to Biff's propensity to steal, to drive without a licence and to shirk work in favour of sport. The reality is that Biff has turned out to be an unremarkable ranch hand and petty thief, drifting from one low-paid job to the next and ending up in jail.

Willy had prided himself on the **'training'** that he had given his boys, bringing them up to be **'rugged, well-liked, all-around'** and delighting in Ben's approval of them as **'a couple of fearless characters'** *(Act One)*. Willy recalls Charley's warning that **'the jails are full of fearless characters'**, laughing at him with Ben and later calling Charley's son, a **'worm'** *(Act One)*. In the real-time scene in Charley's office, Willy discovers that Bernard has grown into a fine young man with a career as a successful lawyer and treating his father with respect and consideration. Maddeningly for Willy, Charley admits that he never told Bernard what to do or took any interest in his son's education or future.

Miller also invites comparison between the older generational brothers Ben and Willy and between Willy's sons Biff and Happy.

Like Ben, Biff has left home and 'wanders', although, unlike Ben, he has yet to strike it rich. Biff is a drifter rather than a fortune-hunter but his instinct to live and work with nature is derived in part from his father, a side of himself that Willy has not allowed to develop – a man who is excited by **'the grand outdoors'** *(Act Two)*, who regrets not going to Alaska to manage Ben's timberlands and who is never happier than when working **'with his hands'** *(Requiem)*.

Happy is more like his father in terms of his dream of selling, making money and becoming **'number-one man'** *(Requiem)*. No longer living at home, he nevertheless is in regular contact with his parents, but spends his time indulging himself and seeking meaningless sexual encounters with girls he has no intention of marrying.

Activity 4

Which of Willy's qualities does each of his sons appear to have inherited, as presented by Miller? Find a quotation to support each trait.

Sibling rivalry

Miller also presents sibling rivalry as a theme in the play. Although, strictly speaking, Ben is dead and an illusion, he is still capable of being dismissive of his little brother, telling him contemptuously, **'With one gadget he [father] made more in a week than a man like you could make in a lifetime'** *(Act One)*. Willy evidently worships his construct of his older brother Ben and appears impervious to his little put-downs. However, he is constantly measuring himself against him and finding himself lacking.

The rivalry between Biff and Happy is also complicated and tinged with Happy's hero-worship of Biff. While Happy is more successful than Biff in material terms, he dreams of sharing a future with his elder brother and becoming Loman Brothers.

He is not prepared to join Biff as a rancher, however, despite being excited by the prospect, asking matter-of-factly, **'what can you make out there?'** *(Act One)* However, Happy's idea about selling sports equipment and creating a Loman brand brings the Act One to an optimistic and harmonious end.

All harmony between Happy and Biff is dissipated in Act Two, though. Biff accuses Happy of not giving **'a good goddam about'** Willy to which Happy angrily retorts, **'Me? Who goes away? Who runs off and –'** *(Act Two)*. The brothers continue to argue as the play reaches its climax with Happy defending himself against Biff's accusations, saying **'We always told the truth!'** *(Act Two)* After Biff turns on him, Happy is cowed into silence.

The rift between the brothers is not healed and we see, in Requiem, their estrangement has crystallized around their competing constructs of the right dream, with Biff ready to return to ranching and Happy determined to stay in the city and **'beat this racket'**. Biff has learned something about himself and is determined to be true to it, while Happy, like his father perhaps, is still in denial and chooses to pursue Willy's dream of coming out **'number-one man'**.

Identity and the significance of names

Questions of identity have been the stuff of tragedies for centuries. Many a tragedy concludes with the hero finally recognizing himself for the flawed human being that he is and accepting this newly revealed identity.

Shakespeare's King Lear is sometimes likened to Willy Having abdicated the throne and given all his wealth to his ungrateful daughters, King Lear struggles with the problem of his identity when they mistreat him, crying out in anguish: 'Who is it that can tell me who I am?' *(King Lear*, Act 4, Scene 4). It is a pitiful cry that may well remind us of Willy Loman at the end of Act Two. Willy clings to the identity conferred on him by his role as a salesman and by the name that he is so proud of, reminding Biff at his moment of crisis that, **'I am not a dime a dozen! I am Willy Loman, and you are Biff Loman!'**

In Shakespeare's play, it is the Fool who tells Lear who he has become, telling the former king that he is merely 'Lear's shadow' *(King Lear*, Act 4, Scene 4). In Miller's play, it is Biff who tells his father, **'I am not a leader of men, Willy, and neither are you'** *(Act Two)*. Here Biff shares with his father his complete

Lear becomes a shadow of the king he once was; 2010 Royal Shakespeare Company production of *King Lear*, with Greg Hicks as Lear and Kathryn Hunter as the Fool

reassessment of their characters and perhaps, like the Fool, implies that Willy is a shadow of the man Biff used to think he was.

Thus, only Biff seems secure about who he is in the closing stages of the play and, although it is not a very comforting revelation for him that **'I'm nothing'**, his realization will enable him to develop in the future *(Act Two)*.

Names

While Miller dismissed the notion that he named the central figure Willy Loman to suggest his status in life as a low man, claiming that Willy was named after a character called Lohmann in the expressionist film *The Testament of Dr Mabuse*, there is no avoiding Miller's foregrounding of the notion that a man's name is significant and that he emphasizes the importance of names throughout the play.

The only character in the play who calls Willy by his full name of William is the phantom figure of Ben. Other characters use the diminutive form Willy, which is more of a child's name. Even Biff calls his father Willy in the closing section of Act Two, as he struggles to make him understand something about himself. By using his first name rather than calling him 'Pop', perhaps Biff is reaching out to him as an equal.

Elsewhere, Willy harks on about his own name and about Biff's. When he overhears Biff telling Hap and Linda that **'They've laughed at Dad for years'**, Willy retorts angrily, **'Call out the name Willy Loman and see what happens'** *(Act One)*. Later, Willy boasts to Ben about Biff, telling him, **'when he walks into a business office his name will sound out like a bell and all the doors will open to him'** *(Act Two)*. However, when Biff does wait outside the business office of Bill Oliver, hoping to secure backing for his business plan, he waits for six hours without being seen despite repeatedly **'sending my name in'** *(Act Two)*.

Biff and Happy fantasize about their business project of selling sports equipment but it is their planned name for the brand, Loman Brothers, that fires their imagination.

Key quotation

Two brothers, see? The Loman Brothers. Displays in the Royal Palms – all the hotels. And banners over the ring and the basketball court: 'Loman Brothers'
(Happy, Act One)

When Willy goes to see his boss, Howard persistently calls Willy 'Kid', which appears insulting as a name for a man old enough to be his father. Willy clings to the notion that because he named his boss's child Howard when he was a baby, he deserved better treatment from him. Charley tries to make Willy see that such an idea is illogical: **'Willy, when're you gonna realize that them things don't mean anything? You named him Howard, but you can't sell that. The only thing you got in this world is what you can sell'** *(Act Two)*.

Activity 5

Write a page about the significance of names and how they give characters a sense of identity in *Death of a Salesman*.

Money

Money is both a key theme and a key motif in the play. Biff defines himself as a **'one dollar an hour'** man *(Act Two)* and when Happy is talking about one of his senior colleagues he says, '**...when he walks into the store the waves part in front of him. That's fifty-two thousand dollars a year coming through the revolving door'** *(Act One)*. Biff's inability to earn any 'real' money is what irks Willy so much and, having calculated that both Biff and Happy would be **'five times ahead'** of Bernard in the business world *(Act One)*, he has to face up to the fact that Bernard is a successful lawyer with a glittering career and two boys of his own.

The play features multiple references to bucks, dollars, cents and dimes. There is talk of wealth and fortune; Ben's repeated catchphrase is about being rich and Linda calculates both Willy's income and her housekeeping necessities down to the last cent.

Additionally, we see money physically changing hands on stage several times, especially when Charley is counting out his loans to Willy, but also in the restaurant scene and when Charley and Willy play cards in Act One.

> **Key quotations**
>
> **I'll put my money on Biff.**
> *(Willy, Act One)*
>
> **The man knew what he wanted and went out and got it! Walked into a jungle, and comes out, the age of twenty-one, and he's rich!**
> *(Willy, Act One)*
>
> **Does it take more guts to stand here the rest of my life ringing up a zero?**
> *(Willy, Act Two)*
>
> **I'm one dollar an hour, Willy! I tried seven states and couldn't raise it.**
> *(Biff, Act One)*
>
> **Can you imagine that magnificence with twenty thousand dollars in his pocket?**
> *(Willy, Act Two)*

Activity 6

a) Write a sentence to explain the significance of each of the quotations above.

b) Look for similar references to money, salary, payment and loans, then write an essay plan on the significance of the theme of money in the play.

Travel, distance and geographical location

Another theme of the play relates to travel, distance and location. Willy's father, Ben and Willy himself all travel in order to make money. For example, Ben refers to the great distances that his father travelled in order to make his living selling flutes: **'through Ohio, and Indiana, Michigan, Illinois, and all the Western states'** *(Act One)*. Ben also refers expansively to new continents to be discovered and to distant areas ripe for conquest, such as the jungles of Africa and the timberlands of Alaska. Willy's father's travels take him away from his family forever.

By contrast, although Willy tells the boys about the lure of cities such as Providence, Waterbury, Boston, Portland and Bangor, it is always as a prelude to coming **'straight home!'** *(Act One)*, to being where he feels most comfortable, in his own back yard, where he attempts to live the more domesticated version of the American Dream.

Activity 7

Identify where Ben, Willy, Willy's father, Biff and Happy travel and why. How does this relate to different versions of the American Dream?

Writing about themes

Themes are highlighted by writers in a variety of different ways. Make sure that you consider the following methods:

- identifying a theme in the title of the play
- identifying its substance – what it is about
- themes, such as money or the past, being discussed by the characters
- themes being revealed by the characters' actions, e.g. by competing with siblings
- highlighting or supporting the theme through linguistic techniques such as repeated phrases or motifs, e.g. many references to time and remembering.

In your assessment, you might be asked how Miller presents a theme, e.g. 'How does Miller present the theme of sibling rivalry in *Death of a Salesman*?' This type of question requires you consider the different methods that the playwright has used to convey the theme.

You might be asked to consider the relative importance of a theme, e.g. 'How important do you think the themes of truth and lies are in the play?' To answer this type of question, you should consider how the themes relate to Miller's main purpose and how they compare to other significant themes.

Plays are written for performance either live on stage or filmed for a TV or cinema audience. The performance of a play can only be achieved through collaboration between a director and a cast of actors, supported by designers responsible for setting and props, costume, lighting and sound. The team all work together on the playwright's **script** to find ways of bringing the play to life for an audience.

In the case of *Death of a Salesman*, its overnight success and enduring popularity have often been attributed to the fact that its first production was the result of an inspired collaboration between the playwright Miller, the director Elia Kazan, set and lighting designer Jo Mielziner and composer/sound designer Alex North. Together with a cast of superb actors, they realized Miller's complex vision of the disintegration of Willy's mind and of the subtle interplay between past, present and imagination.

script the written version of the play as used in rehearsals for a performance

Dramatic interpretation

The director's role

Death of a Salesman is probably the most frequently performed of Miller's plays and directors over the past 60 or so years have interpreted and re-interpreted the play.

No two directors will ever make exactly the same decisions about how to present the various characters or about which themes to emphasize. For example, it is possible to direct Linda Loman as the embodiment of wifely virtue and self-effacement, patient with Willy and full of deference. She may be made to appear uninteresting, through her voice, physical movement, costume and make-up.

It is equally possible to portray Linda as ferocious in her love for Willy and in her defence of him to the boys. She can be directed to use her voice to be sarcastic with both Happy and Biff, intolerant of their indifference towards their father's decline and almost dictatorial in her instructions and prohibitions to them. Such an interpretation may also be conveyed through tone of voice, volume and pitch, through movement and stance on stage and through appropriate choice of costume.

It is the director's job to study and re-read the play many times before making crucial decisions about what they want the audience to take away from the performance in terms of character, theme and feeling. For example, should the audience leave the theatre feeling that Willy Loman is indeed a tragic hero or should they see him more as a down-trodden, rather pitiful victim of his own failed dreams or of rabid capitalism? Should the audience feel that Happy is right to defend his father's ambitions to be 'number-one man' or to agree with Biff that Willy had 'the wrong dreams' *(Requiem)*. Should Willy's suicide be seen as a victory or a defeat? These decisions will create an individual interpretation of the play.

Activity 1

Make a list of other aspects of the play that you think are open to a variety of interpretations. These could be related to characters or themes.

The actors

Before rehearsals for a production can begin, the director will have given a great deal of thought to casting the roles because this is a very significant aspect of interpretation. Casting affects the way that audiences respond to individual characters. The director will take into account each actor's physical appearance in terms of their age, ethnicity, build, height, colouring, facial features and vocal qualities to match each role with a suitable actor and create an ensemble of actors who are most likely to be able to deliver the director's vision of the play.

All casting decisions will be based upon whether the director is intending to retain the Brooklyn setting that Miller originally envisaged or to **transpose** the play to another setting. For example, in 1983, Miller directed a Chinese translation of the play in Beijing with an all-Chinese cast. Any transposition needs to be justified in terms of its relevance to the network of relationships, themes and social context as depicted in the original time and setting envisaged by the writer.

> **transposition** in theatre, the creation of a production set in a completely different time period or geographical setting from the original; some plays lend themselves more readily to transposition than others

Activity 2

Imagine you are going to be directing a production of *Death of a Salesman*.

a) Write down the physical and vocal qualities that you would be looking for in the actors that you cast to play the following roles: Willy, Linda, the Woman, Biff, Bernard.

Think about what each actor's age, build and height should be, together with any particular facial features that you consider to be important assets for each role. Think about what each actor's voice should be like, considering the pitch, pace and tone of voice as well as accent.

b) Justify your choices based on evidence from the play.

c) Share your ideas with the rest of your group and discuss all the suggestions made for each character.

Activity 3

Find online clips from the 1966 and 1985 films of *Death of a Salesman*. Compare the very different portrayals of Willy and Biff.

In the 1966 film, shown here, Willy was played by Lee J. Cobb and Biff by George Segal; whereas Dustin Hoffman played Willy and John Malkovitch Biff in the 1985 film

Having selected the 'right' actor for each role, in terms of their appearance and vocal qualities, the director must work with the actors to help them develop their characters and realize the complexity of the roles, while being mindful of not imitating productions that have preceded their own. When we read the play we have to imagine the actors' tone of voice, movement, gesture and handling of **props**, whereas when we are watching a production, the actors demonstrate all of these aspects in their performances.

With the exception of Ben, most of the characters show a range of emotions throughout the play, but they express these emotions, as we have seen, using colloquial language, as well as occasionally repetitive and sometimes unfinished lines of text. In the theatre, the meaning and emotion behind these half-lines and incomplete utterances must be conveyed through spatial relationships on stage and non-verbal communication, which involves the following aspects:

- use of space
- use of pause
- eye contact and eye line
- facial expression
- body language
- tears/laughter
- physical contact
- use of props.

Non-verbal reactions are especially useful in conveying the characters' reactions to unfolding events, as well as the subtle shifts in their moods and attitudes, to the audience.

A particular challenge in *Death of a Salesman* is to make clear the differences between the characters as they appear in the present action and how they appear in Willy Loman's memories and imaginings. Shifts in time will be signalled through the appearance of the characters, through the use of costume and wigs (for Linda, certainly), and through acting dynamics.

prop a moveable object used on stage by the actors

Setting design

The stage design as set out in Miller's stage directions for the play is a challenging one for any designer as it is expressed so impressionistically:

> **Key quotation**
>
> *A melody is heard, played upon a flute. It is small and fine, telling of grass and trees and the horizon. The curtain rises.*
>
> *Before us is the Salesman's house. We are aware of towering, angular shapes behind it, surrounding it on all sides. Only the blue light of the sky falls upon the house and forestage; the surrounding area shows an angry glow of orange. As more light appears, we see a solid vault of apartment houses around the small, fragile-seeming home. An air of the dream clings to the place, a dream rising out of reality.*
> *(Act One)*

Certainly, the concept *'an air of the dream'* appears imprecise as a clue to a stage designer, who must create a three-dimensional and fully functioning set for actors to enter and exit from and inhabit in their roles.

For the play's premiere in February 1949, at the Morosco Theatre in New York, the designer Jo Mielziner was responsible for the set and lighting. He created a set on three levels with:

- the kitchen at stage level
- Willy's and Linda's bedroom raised slightly above stage level
- the boys' bedroom, set back, above and as if behind the kitchen.

The original stage set, designed by Jo Mielziner for the Morosco Theatre, New York, 1949

There were no walls between the rooms. A staircase went from a hall area by the front door of the Loman's house to the boys' room.

Behind the outline of the house hung a fine fabric gauze. When lit from the front, the gauze showed two large trees, bathed in a soft golden light, suggesting the Lomans' house as it was in Willy's memory. When the gauze was back-lit, it illuminated the image of towering apartment buildings, hemming in the little house beneath and signalling real time.

Scenes not set in the Lomans' home, such as those in Howard's office, the yard where Linda hung her washing or in the restaurant, were created in a large area on the fore-stage. The actors would bring on portable props to signify the location.

Other designers have tackled the stage design in different ways. For example, in a 1996 revival of *Death of a Salesman* at the National Theatre in London, designer Fran Thompson responded to the concept that much of the action of the play takes place in Willy's mind. The design consisted of a sawn-off tree trunk at the centre of a series of concentric circles. The actors remained on stage throughout the play but were on the outer edge of the circle when not performing in the scene, coming forward towards centre stage as they entered the real-time action or Willy's imaginings.

Costume

Because the play is set very clearly in the social milieu of the Loman family in 1940s New York, there is limited scope for variety of interpretation when it comes to costume design and most directors have chosen to set the play in its original context. Whatever period or location is selected by the director, however, the costumes need to be authentic to that period and setting to reflect the realistic nature of the drama. In a production that adheres to Miller's initial conception of the play, the boys, Linda and the Woman in the memory scenes need to be wearing clothes authentic to the late 1920s.

Miller was quite specific in his stage directions, as well as in textual references about some of the costumes and/or props required for certain characters in his original production. For example:

- **From the right, Willy Loman, the Salesman, enters, carrying two large sample cases [...] He is past sixty years of age, dressed quietly.** *(Act One)*
- **Young Biff and Young Happy appear from the direction Willy was addressing. Happy carries rags and a pail of water. Biff, wearing a sweater with a block 'S', carries a football.** *(Act One)*
- **Uncle Ben, carrying a valise and an umbrella, enters the forestage from around the right corner of the house. He is a stolid man, in his sixties, with a moustache and an authoritative air. He is utterly certain of his destiny, and there is an aura of far places about him. He enters exactly as Willy speaks.** *(Act One)*

Ben, played by Guy Paul, wears a sophisticated white suit in the 2015 Royal Shakespeare Company production

Costume design for the character of Ben has frequently offered more opportunity for invention. Some designers have dressed Ben in a conventional double-breasted suit with matching waistcoat, flashy watch chain and signet ring – all authentic to the period of his great successes in the early part of the 20th century. Others have suggested his unrealistic or other-worldly aspect by having such a costume all in white or spectral grey, with white/grey shoes and hat to match.

Activity 4

Re-read the specific suggestions that Miller made in the text for costumes and props for individual characters. Write a sentence for each one, explaining the significance of these ideas to the play as a whole.

Music

Music is vital in creating an appropriate and ever-changing mood to the play. In the original production, Alex North composed musical **leitmotifs** associated with individual characters and to create different emotions for the audience.

The play opens with the flute playing an evocative melody suggestive of the past and intended to remind the audience of Willy's father, the salesman who made and sold his own flutes before abandoning Willy to a permanent state of feeling 'kind of temporary' about himself *(Act One)*.

leitmotif a musical phrase or melody associated with specific characters or ideas and repeated in the course of a performance

89

The music that Alex North composed for Ben was more lively and often played on the trumpet – a suitable instrument to suggest his pride in his professional success.

North also used the melody of the music that Linda hums to Willy at the end of Act One to soothe him to sleep to create an ironic counterpoint when introducing the Woman, when it was played as a distorted jazz-style overture.

Finally, for the teenage Biff and Hap, North composed the *'gay'* harmonies *(Act Two)*, described in the text when they appeared in Willy's memory. This use of these harmonies worked a little like a film score to encourage the audience to empathize with Willy's tumultuous emotions during the course of the play.

Production history

It has been stated by commentators many times that, at any one time since Miller wrote the play, some theatre company, somewhere on the planet, is performing *Death of a Salesman*.

Two of the more recent productions in the English-speaking world are the 1999 Broadway revival, starring Brian Dennehy as Willy with Elizabeth Franz as Linda, to celebrate the play's 50th anniversary and the Royal Shakespeare Company's (RSC) centenary celebration of Miller's birth in their 2015 production at Stratford, when Anthony Sher played Willy and Harriet Walters played Linda.

Both productions garnered impressive reviews from the critics. The Dennehy version was more original in terms of staging, which utilized two large **revolves** to move from location to location, and in the interpretation of the relationship between Willy and Linda. Elizabeth Franz's performance as Linda was unusual in emphasizing the sexual dimension in her love for her husband rather than the semi-maternal one usually demonstrated.

> **revolve stage** a stage with a large circular area that can be rotated either as part of the action or to reveal new settings

The RSC production was much more conventional. Its major strength was in the casting of the two lead characters. Directly after playing Willy Loman, Sher played the central role in Shakespeare's *King Lear*, also at the RSC, drawing direct comparisons between the tragic roles of Willy Loman and King Lear.

Stephen Brimson Lewis' design in the 2015 production was just as the text describes, with one little house dwarfed by *'towering, angular'* apartment buildings around it *(Act One)*. The Loman home was a spectral grey, almost invisible, with Willy and Linda almost blending into the background. The wooden structure was surrounded by red brick and metal. Critics complained that it did not conjure up Miller's idea of *'a dream rising out of reality'* *(Act One)* and that it did not exploit the technology of the 21st century to realize Miller's expressionist vision.

You may find it helpful to refer to two productions that have been turned into successful television or film versions, and which are accessible on DVD or the

Internet. The first of these, the 1966 CBS television version, stars Lee J. Cobb as Willy and Mildred Dunnock as Linda. Both of these actors had been in the original stage production 17 years earlier. George Segal plays Biff and Gene Wilder makes a brief appearance as Bernard. The play was adapted to fit the TV time slot available and attracted 20 million viewers when it was first shown.

Being a TV rather than a stage production allowed for more realistic settings, nevertheless it still retains elements of expressionism with the retention of the no-walls principle in the Loman house and the scenes set in the yard being shot against a backdrop of dazzling white.

Miller worked with the director Alex Segal to cut the text for television, with a resulting reduction in the complexity of effects created. For example, Happy's explanation of his compulsive womanizing and his susceptibility to bribe-taking is cut as is the substance of his interaction with Miss Forsythe in the restaurant scene. Many more of the cuts involved Linda's role. She doesn't appear in the scene where Ben tricks Biff into submission in the mock fight; she doesn't remind Willy about Dave Singleman when Ben dangles the prospect of a job in Alaska before Willy; she doesn't ensure that Willy has his glasses, handkerchief and saccharine when he sets off to see Howard about a New York job. In short, her role is diminished and as a result she becomes a more traditional supportive wife than Miller wrote in the play.

Another accessible version is the 1985 televized production starring Dustin Hoffman as Willy with John Malkovich in the role of Biff. This was a 'translation' of a stage version into the medium of film. While the stage version had utilized a revolving stage to accommodate the various shifts in location in the play, for the screen version, different sets were used and then edited into the film, with the overall result being more realistic than expressionistic.

One striking difference between Lee J. Cobb's performance and that of Dustin Hoffman is in the physical size of the actors. While Cobb was a big man, with a broad build and long limbs, Hoffman is small and almost bird-like. Miller adapted the script to fit the different actors' physicalities. When Cobb tells Linda that his looks have attracted jokes, he refers to having been compared to a walrus; when Hoffman delivers the line he was being compared to a shrimp.

Hoffman's performance is very distinctive. As a method actor, his preparation was meticulous and he was edgy, nervous and unpredictable in his mood swings from the very beginning. Malkovich was also a very effective Biff, whose final scene with Willy was made even more poignant by Biff kissing Willy after telling him, 'Will you take that phony dream and burn it before something happens?' (Act Two).

Once again, some of the play text was cut. For example, the telephone call between Linda and Biff was cut completely. Biff and Happy's conversation in Act One about their lives and expectations was also quite heavily cut, resulting in less of a sense of their contrasting dreams.

Activity 5

Watch the 1966 and 1985 film versions of *Death of a Salesman* in full.

Write a critic's article, comparing and contrasting the strengths and weaknesses of the two films in relation to Miller's full text. Use the grid below to help structure your work.

	Plays performed on stage	Film/TV versions of plays
Setting	The action of the play must be depicted in a single stage space, although the space may be transformed into a series of separate settings using stage mechanics to create the illusion of different locations.	The action of the play may be depicted in any number of different locations – both interior and exterior – and in any part of the world. These locations may appear to be real.
Time	A stage play follows the chronology (time sequence) as written by the playwright. *Death of a Salesman* involves dreams and memories that all occur in real time.	A film may include flashbacks and flash forwards.
The text	Most plays are produced more or less in their entirety with few cuts made to the original text.	Directors often cut sections of text, preferring to replace them with film images of what was described in the text.
Action	References to events that occur offstage are used to give the audience the necessary information to help them understand the story.	Action may be portrayed in the film, becoming a fully realized part of the story.
Characters	Characters that do not appear on stage may be referred to or described by the onstage actors.	The director may choose to use actors to portray these characters in the film, dispensing with descriptions.
Audience view	From their seats in the auditorium, the audience, who can see the whole stage, may choose whom or what to watch.	The director chooses every shot of the film; the audience must watch the character selected by the director, so their experience is more closely shaped by the director.
Actors	Sections of the audience may be some distance away from the stage, so the actors must project their voices and ensure that their gestures and facial expressions are clearly defined. The audience listens to the dialogue to make sense of the play and understand each character's feelings.	A film actor can be more subtle; the director can choose close-ups to highlight significant moments and facial expressions. The director can also choose to use a voice-over to explain the inner thoughts of a particular character.
Performance	As the actors and action is live, no two performances (even by the same cast) are ever identical.	The film performance is captured forever; it never changes.

Activity 6

If you were directing a production of *Death of a Salesman*, which of the themes might you want to highlight for your audience? Write a page about why your chosen theme is the most important one, in your view.

Writing about performance

When you are answering a question about *Death of a Salesman* in your assessment, remember to write about Miller's intentions for the audience, rather than for the reader, as it is the audience that the playwright is addressing. Even if you do not have an opportunity to see the play at the theatre, you need to imagine what the scenes would look like on stage as well as the effects that are created for the audience as the action unfolds.

Remember, also, that you must write about the play as Miller wrote it and not be tempted to make reference to film or TV versions that you may have seen, where the director has chosen to cut or alter lines to fit in with their interpretation, unless asked to take this approach in your assessment.

There are numerous different critical readings of *Death of a Salesman*, a play that has attracted the attention of both theatrical and scholarly criticism since its first production in 1949.

Social, political or Marxist perspectives

Critics who analyse texts in terms of their social or political concerns normally focus on social and economic issues. *Death of a Salesman* has attracted a wealth of Marxist criticism on account of its depiction of a society dependent upon consumerism, which is both a by-product of a capitalist society and a fundamental aspect of the American Dream. As a salesman of an unspecified line of goods, as well as being an avid consumer of products (refrigerator, vacuum cleaner, cars, hammock, punch-bag) Willy is both a victim and a functionary of the capitalist society so deplored by Marx.

> **Marxism and Marxist criticism**
>
> Marxist criticism adopts the perspective on society developed by the socialist philosophers Karl Marx (1818–1883) and Friedrich Engels (1820–1895). Marxism embraces a worldview that depicts workers as the exploited tools of their employers. Marxism also identifies the negative impact that capitalism has on people who throw all their energies into acquiring material wealth. Marx believed that people who focus exclusively on making money, and who ignore other human values such as family, comradeship and love, become alienated from their own humanity.

Eleanor Clark, a drama critic writing in response to the first production of *Death of Salesman* sees the play as blatantly pro-Marxist and condemns it for being so:

> It is, of course, the capitalist system that has done Willy in; the scene in which he is brutally fired after some forty years with the firm comes straight from the party line literature of the thirties, and the idea emerges [...] that it is our particular form of money economy that has bred the absurdly false ideals of both father and sons.
>
> (Eleanor Clark, quoted in *Miller: a study of his plays*, Dennis Welland, 1979)

Another critic, Jeffrey Mason offers a challenge to previous readings of Miller as a socialist playwright. In his book, *The Stone Tower: the political theatre of Arthur Miller* (2008), Mason creates a distinction between social and political drama, and claims that while social drama explores man's relationship with society, political drama is more concerned with raising consciousness and inciting activism.

Mason concludes that the play has never incited an audience to rebel against the class structure or against the capitalist system that restricts Willy's advancement because we see Willy entirely in personal terms.

This view was countered by Raymond Williams in his 1973 essay on Miller, where he refers specifically to Marx's theory of alienation:

 I think in the end it is not Willy Loman as a man, but the image of the Salesman that predominates. The social figure sums up the theme of alienation, for this is a man who from selling things has passed to selling himself and has become, in effect, a commodity which like other commodities will at a certain point be economically discarded.

(Raymond Williams, *Drama from Ibsen to Brecht*, 1973)

 Activity 1

Use some of the following quotations to support or to challenge the idea that the play can be read as an attack on capitalism.

I put thirty-four years into this firm, Howard, and now I can't pay my insurance! You can't eat the orange and throw the peel away – a man is not a piece of fruit! *(Willy, Act Two)*

No, but it's a business, kid, and everybody's gotta pull his own weight. [...] 'Cause you gotta admit, business is business. *(Howard, Act Two)*

The only thing you got in this world is what you can sell. And the funny thing is that you're a salesman, and you don't know that. *(Charley, Act Two)*

I stopped in the middle of that building and I saw – the sky. I saw the things that I love in this world. The work and the food and time to sit and smoke. And I looked at the pen and said to myself, what the hell am I grabbing this for? Why am I trying to become what I don't want to be? *(Biff, Act Two)*

I gotta show some of those pompous, self-important executives over there that Hap Loman can make the grade. *(Happy, Act One)*

Once in my life I would like to own something outright before it's broken! I'm always in a race with the junkyard! [...] They time those things. They time them so when you finally paid for them, they're used up. *(Willy, Act Two)*

Shipping clerk, salesman, business of one kind and another. And it's a measly manner of existence [...] To devote your whole life to keeping stock, or making phone calls, or selling or buying [...] And always to have to get ahead of the next fella. *(Biff, Act One)*

Perhaps it is worth allowing Miller to have the last word on how far the play should be interpreted on strictly Marxist or socialist principles:

 In today's America the term 'social play' brings up images which are historically conditioned, very recent, and, I believe, only incidentally pertinent to a fruitful conception of the drama. The term indicates to us an attack, an arraignment [putting on trial] of society's evils such as Ibsen allegedly invented and was later taken up by left-wing playwrights whose primary interest was the exposure of capitalism for the implied benefit of **socialism** or communism. The concept is tired and narrow, but its worst effect has been to confuse a whole generation of playwrights, audiences and theatre workers.

(Arthur Miller, 'On social plays', quoted in *The Theatre Essays of Arthur Miller*, edited by Robert A. Martin, 1978)

socialism an ideology based on the belief that society should be run on egalitarian principles, e.g. with cooperative ownership of businesses, where profits are shared amongst all the people involved

Feminist perspectives

Feminist criticism relates to the exploration of a writer's depiction of women within their fictional or dramatic works. Feminist critics tend to examine one or more of four main areas associated with the presentation of women in literature:

- gender difference
- gender inequality
- oppression of women
- objectification of women, when they are viewed as objects to serve men rather than as individuals in their own right.

Linda, played by Mildred Dunnock, plays the dutiful, smiling housewife to Fredric March's Willy in the 1951 film

Death of a Salesman has been subject to intense scrutiny by feminist critics in the past 25 years, much of the attention focusing on Linda's role in the play.

Linda is traditionally seen as the archetypal supporting wife and loving mother to her two boys. Willy calls her **'my foundation and my support'** *(Act One)* and she is frequently interpreted by critics and by actresses as a nurturing figure, massaging Willy's ego, over-looking his deficiencies and valiantly coping with his ever-diminishing income.

Guerin Bliquez offered a different view in an article about Linda's role in the publication, 'Modern Drama' in 1967:

Mrs. Willy Loman has a more forceful role in *Death of a Salesman* than most commentators have thus far noted. To overlook the part she plays in her husband's pathetic downfall is to miss one of the most profound levels in Arthur Miller's subtle structuring of his tragedy. Linda's facility for prodding Willy to his doom is what gives the play its direction and its impetus.

(Guerin Bliquez, 'Linda's role in *Death of a Salesman*', in *Modern Drama*, Winter 1967, Volume 10, Number 4

Bliquez argues that Miller intended the audience to criticize Linda for acquiescing both in Willy's life and in his death:

Acquiescence is passive. Understanding plays no part. A wife cannot acquiesce morally to a husband's serious faults. If Linda accepts Willy for what he is shown to be, she accepts a liar, a cheat, and a pompous fraud. Such attributes cannot be explained away, as Linda tries to do, by her husband's exhaustion [...] To acquiesce in all of Willy's weaknesses is to be a failure as a wife and mother, and to share in the responsibility of her husband's fall.

(Guerin Bliquez, as above)

Activity 2

Find examples in the text where Linda's acceptance of Willy's dishonesty or of his weakness is demonstrated to the audience. Use these examples to support an essay plan for the question: 'How far do you agree that Linda is partly responsible for Willy's suicide in *Death of a Salesman*?'

Nevertheless, other feminist critics have argued that Linda is a victim of the patriarchal society that existed at the time the play was written, in as much as she acquiesces in a system that denigrates and exploits women. Both Janet Balakian, in her essay 'Beyond the Male Locker Room: *Death of a Salesman* from a feminist perspective', and Kay Stanton, in her essay 'Women and the American Dream of *Death of a Salesman*', see the play as an expression of how men depend upon their subjugation and exploitation of women to maintain their foothold in their quest for advancement.

For feminists, Linda is defined by the house that she never leaves – not even to accompany her husband to dinner with their sons – and by the domestic appliances needed to fulfil her role as housewife/unpaid help. The faulty refrigerator, the washing machine, the vacuum cleaner and the baskets full of washing that she carries in the memory scenes are all symbols of Linda's domestic drudgery and lack of 'meaningful' work.

Feminists would argue that Willy robs Linda of a 'voice' in the family. He frequently interrupts her, or expostulates rudely at her opinions, when she has the temerity to voice them.

The fact that Willy cheats on Linda is another indication that he **'Never had an ounce of respect for you'**, as Biff points out *(Act One)*. And Freudian critics may also see Willy's gift of stockings to the Woman, while Linda must mend her old ones, as a sign of sexual abandonment. Willy's claim to want to **'kiss the life outa you'** *(Act One)*, when they are apart, is immediately exposed by Miller as meaningless, as the line is underscored by the laughter of the Woman with whom Willy was having a regular sexual liaison.

Despite Linda defining herself as being part of Willy, telling Biff that, **'if you don't have any feeling for him, then you can't have any feeling for me'** *(Act One)*, she is oblivious to his infidelity, continuing to support and admire him despite his flaws.

Both Linda and the Woman (who is too insignificant in Willy's memory to have a name) are objectified by Willy in a feminist reading of the play. Linda serves the function of servant and mother figure to Willy in the real-time scenes, waxing the kitchen floor, helping him off with his shoes and his jacket, mending his jacket and singing him to sleep. The Woman is nothing more than a sex object to Willy. He behaves crudely towards her, **'slapping her bottom'**, kissing her **'roughly'** and making risqué jokes about keeping her **'pores open'** *(Act One)*. Later, in an attempt to save face with his 17-year-old son, he bundles the Woman out into the hall, semi-naked, like a football, as she remarks. As both these sequences emanate from Willy's memory, they represent his sexist attitude towards the Woman fairly accurately.

Feminist critics also point out how Biff and Happy demonstrate similarly dismissive attitudes towards girls and women. While appearing to revere their mother, as **'Somebody with character, with resistance'** *(Act One)*, both Happy and Biff indulge in meaningless sexual relationships with women who they both objectify and appear to revile.

Happy's recollection in Act One about his first sexual partner, described by Biff as 'that big Betsy something' is completely derogatory and dehumanizing: 'Boy, there was a pig!' Happy describes the women that he and Biff have been with as 'creatures' rather than people (Act One), and he boasts to his brother about 'ruining' the fiancées of his work colleagues, and then attending their weddings. Biff also describes the girls as 'most gorgeous I've had in years' (Act One), objectifying the women into 'consumable' commodities. Happy refers to his sexual conquests being 'like bowling or something. I just keep knockin' them over and it doesn't mean anything', comparing the women to inanimate pins (Act One).

Happy, more than Biff, appears to be completely misogynistic. It is Happy who we see lying to Miss Forsythe in the restaurant, flattering her with empty compliments and ordering her to find another girl for Biff's purposes. Happy is prepared to abandon his father in the pursuit of 'Strudel' (Act One) – another demeaning description of women, comparing them to edible objects.

Most feminist critics would agree with Janet Balakian, who maintains that the play depicts America 'through the male gaze' of Willy Loman.

Activity 3

'How far does your reading of Death of a Salesman convince you that the play depicts America in the 1940s "through the male gaze" of Willy Loman?'

a) Write an introduction in response to the question.

b) Use bullet points to plan a full answer.

Freudian and other psychoanalytical perspectives

Psychoanalytical critical perspectives take the theories that psychoanalysts such as Sigmund Freud and Carl Jung applied to their patients and then attempt to apply them to the fictional or dramatized characters in novels and plays. This practice is accepted as a legitimate branch of modern critical theory.

Sigmund Freud and Carl Jung

Sigmund Freud (1856–1939) was an Austrian neurologist and founder of psychoanalysis, who created an entirely new approach to the understanding of the human personality. He is regarded as one of the most influential – and controversial – thinkers of his time.

Carl Jung (1865–1961) was a Swiss psychologist and psychoanalyst who was heavily influenced by Freud during his early career. Later he rejected some of Freud's major theories, notably his focus on the Oedipus complex, a boy's tendency to have sexual feelings toward his mother while wanting to replace his father in her affections. Jung developed his own psychoanalytical theories, primarily the process of individuation, which is how Jung described 'accomplishment of the Self'.

Although Miller rejected the validity of this kind of approach to his plays, arguing that much of the psychoanalytical criticism of his work ran counter to his original intentions as a writer, Freudian critics would argue that the writer is not always conscious of their intentions and is not best placed to interpret their own work.

One insightful study is provided in *Psychology and Arthur Miller* by psychology Professor Richard Evans (1969). Based on interviews with Miller, Evans applies formal concepts of psychology, including Freudian concepts of personality, to Miller's plays.

In brief, Freudian theory is based on the power of the conscious and the unconscious mind. For Freud, the unconscious represents all those hidden forces, desires and fears that cause us to do things without us knowing the reason why. These mental processes are inaccessible to the conscious mind but influence judgements, feelings and behaviour.

Much psychoanalytical theory revolves around family structures and the inter-relationships and conflicts between parents and their children, and between siblings. For this reason, *Death of a Salesman* has attracted a great deal of critical attention from a psychoanalytical perspective.

In a psychoanalytical reading of one of the many strands of the play, Willy uses defence mechanisms (psychological ways in which the unconscious protects itself against painful experiences) in order to avoid facing any of his problems. His principal method of avoiding his problems is through regression, returning to an earlier level of psychological development. In order to avoid the present, Willy re-lives past events in his mind. Like dreams, according to Freud, regressive states usually hold some symbolic meaning coming from the unconscious.

Willy, his dreams blighted by his failure within the social reality that he inhabits, can be seen to have damaged his sons by passing on the same values that have denied him a sense of satisfaction in his achievements. Neither son has escaped psychological damage. All his life, Happy has had to compete with Biff for Willy's attention. To compensate for being overlooked by his father, Happy emulates Willy, both in his adoption of the dream of business success and his need for sexual gratification.

Willy's memories reveal his guilt over betraying Linda with the Woman and the significance of the stockings; Fredric March as Willy and Claire Carleton as the Woman in the 1951 film

Biff's understanding of his own identity collapses in the hotel room in Boston. For the first time, Biff sees his father for who he is, rather than for what he projects. In turn, this transforms Biff from being Willy's 'golden' son into a boy who knows his father's secret and is a threat to Willy's own self-image of beloved husband and ideal father. The father–son relationship is changed irrevocably, although Willy is in denial about this, a defence mechanism in which he intellectually denies what is actually true. Just as in Freud's model of the Oedipus complex, Biff begins to hate his father, (possibly wishing him dead), and he turns passionately to his mother – his 'pal'.

Until the revelation in the hotel room, Willy had been projecting his dreams onto Biff and living vicariously through him and his achievements. Subsequently, Biff's failure to 'make good' in the business world is reflected in Willy's diminishing success.

Activity 4

Use the Internet to find alternative psychoanalytical readings of different plot strands from the play, such as:

- the rivalry between Willy and Ben

- Willy's yearning for a father figure

- the father–son relationship between Charley and Bernard.

Writing about critical views

When writing about *Death of a Salesman*, you may wish to support your ideas about the play by referring to critical views and perspectives. Alternatively, you may choose to outline your reasons for disagreeing either with an individual critic or with a particular school of criticism such as a feminist or Marxist reading of the play. In order to offer an informed, yet personal, view of the play, consider the following advice:

- Read around the text as widely as you can and make notes as you do so. Make sure you know which critic has said what and how it has been justified.

- Read critical opinions that conflict with one another or with your own view of the play and think about how you could defend each one.

- Choose a section of text and apply different critical approaches to it.

- Always acknowledge ideas that you have gleaned from other writers and explain how far you agree with them.

Exam skills

Make sure that you are fully prepared for the challenges of the assessment by following these practical steps.

Step 1: Make sure you know the play really well

Death of a Salesman is quite a short play but its structure and plot demand careful attention, so you should try to read it at least four times and listen to or watch good versions that are available on DVD, on the internet or in the theatre. As you re-read the play, make your own notes under the following headings:

- Plot and structure
- Context
- Characters
- Language
- Themes
- Performance
- Critical reception.

Step 2: Revise effectively

- Go back through this book and check that you have completed all the activities.
- Re-read the key quotations from the play and learn as many as you can.
- Re-read any critical essays or articles that you have used during your study of *Death of a Salesman*.

Activity 1

Prepare for extract-based responses by opening the play randomly. Re-read the passage, annotating or noting what you observe about:

- characters
- themes
- language
- dramatic presentation
- how what happens moves on the plot
- the context
- any relevant critical interpretation
- the significance of this extract to the play as a whole.

Activity 2

a) Prepare for writing about characters by compiling a spider diagram for each character in the play, including branches on:

- themes associated with them
- interpretations of their character
- parallels with other characters
- language and imagery associated with them.

b) Look back through the play and find quotations to support each point on your spider diagram.

Activity 3

a) Prepare for writing about themes, choosing one of the following themes and writing about its importance in the play:

- the American Dream
- truth and lies
- loyalty and betrayal
- sibling rivalry
- memory and anticipation.

b) Repeat the task for other themes.

Tips for assessment

Whether you choose to use lists or diagrams as you plan your answers, it is a good idea to number your ideas so that you work through them in a methodical way. Tick each point once you have incorporated it into your answer so that you avoid repeating yourself or missing it out of your answer completely.

Step 3: Improve your exam technique: types of question

If you are sitting an exam on your set text, working on exam technique can make a real difference to your overall grade.

Make sure that you know which type of question you will face – essay-style, extract-based or comparative. Below are some examples of the different question types that you may be faced with in your exam.

Essay-style questions

Most essay-style questions ask you to write about subtleties of:

- plot (the events that take place in the play and how they are presented)
- structure (how events are organized)
- characters
- themes.

You may also be asked questions about how the writer uses language, about form and genre, as well as about critical perspectives and/or dramatic methods.

Whatever the question, you should also expect to demonstrate your understanding of Miller's use of language, structure and form.

Here are some typical essay-style questions, with key words and phrases underlined. This is followed by a brief explanation of what each question requires. When you first read a question, always underline the key words to make sure you know exactly which direction to take your answer in.

> How does Miller succeed in persuading the audience that Linda is partly responsible for Willy's death?

This question on character requires an examination of Miller's dramatic methods (how) and an appreciation of the writer at work (persuading the audience of Linda's responsibility). It needs more than an examination of Miller's methods in presenting Linda's character, although these methods are relevant, as it has a particular focus upon her responsibility for Willy death.

Because the question only refers to Linda being 'partly responsible' for Willy's death, you may like to suggest other reasons for his death, including, for example:

- the loss of his job and self-respect
- his increasing paranoia, as evidenced by his hallucinations
- his consciousness of the failure of the American Dream to bring success to him and his sons
- his decision to sacrifice himself for Biff's future.

Activity 4

Find quotations from the play to support the bullet points in answer to the question on page 104 about how Linda is presented.

> *Death of a Salesman* has been described as a play <u>about memories</u>. <u>How far do you agree</u> with this description?

This theme-based question is about the nature of the play as a whole. 'How far do you agree… ?' means that you should weigh up the evidence for agreeing (or disagreeing) with the description and consider, if you do agree, whether that agreement is total or partial. You should provide evidence to support your views. A good way to approach this type of question is to consider the appropriateness of the statement in relation to plot, structure, characters, themes, language and imagery.

Extract-based questions

For extract-based questions you should look at past or specimen paper questions to familiarize yourself with the precise demands of your exam. You will need to have plenty of practice in reading extracts carefully, paying close attention to language as well as to the action that occurs in the extract.

When writing answers based on an extract, use a pen or highlighter to underline key words or phrases in the extract that strike you as important. It can also be helpful to make brief notes in the margin to remind you why you picked out these words.

Step 4: Improve your exam technique: answering the question

Always try to think ahead before you start writing. In an exam, you need to plan quickly. Don't spend more than about six or seven minutes on a plan. However, thinking and planning ahead will help you to:

- target the precise demands of the question
- structure your answer logically, starting with the most important ones
- avoid missing out points that are crucial to your argument
- include appropriate quotations.

Plans may take a number of forms. However, a brief list is often the most helpful as it allows you to put your ideas into a logical sequence. Develop your answer step by step, building your argument by referring to precise moments from the extract or wider play. Use paragraphs to structure your response and allocate at least one paragraph to each of the points that you are making.

Tips for assessment

- Always write a brief introduction to your answer that signals to the examiner that you have understood the task and that you are about to address it head on. Use the key words from the question to help you.

- It is equally important to conclude your answer emphatically, returning to the terms of the question. You should not use your final paragraph to summarize your argument but to finalize it.

- Always support your answer with short, relevant quotations from the play.

Step 5: Improve your exam technique: using quotations

The most effective way to use a quotation to support your argument is to embed it into your own grammatically correct sentences. For example, in an answer to a question about Willy's mercurial nature, a student might write:

> At the beginning of Act Two, Miller presents Willy in optimistic mood, he looks 'rested' as he anticipates 'a change' for Biff and looks forward to a time when he and Linda will have 'a little place out in the country'. This is one of the few times in the play where Willy appears to be relaxed. Moments later Miller shows us that Willy is agitated again, cursing, 'That goddamn Studebaker' for being so unreliable and costly, and demonstrating his mercurial temperament.

Sample questions

Essay-style questions

1 Explore the view that Willy's mental state has been caused by his inability to reconcile competing versions of the American Dream. Remember to support your answer with reference to Miller's dramatic methods.

2 Consider the significance of the different settings in *Death of a Salesman*. In what ways is each setting appropriate to the action that takes place there?

3 Explore Miller's opinion that 'the common man is as apt a subject for tragedy in its highest sense as kings' as it applies to *Death of a Salesman*.

4

How does Miller present the theme of memory in *Death of a Salesman*?

5

'Although they are relatively minor characters within the action, Charley and Bernard perform vital roles within *Death of a Salesman*.' Explain how far you agree with this statement and assess the importance of these characters to Miller's overall message.

6

Miller's use of language in *Death of a Salesman* has sometimes been criticized as uninspiring and unpoetic. How would you defend the play from this charge? Support your answer with close reference to the text.

7

Miller is often accused of presenting the women in *Death of a Salesman* through the 'male gaze' of Willy Loman. Explore Miller's reasons for presenting the women in the play as he does. You should support your answer with reference to different interpretations.

8

Do you agree that there is more to *Death of a Salesman* than a study of consumerism? Justify your opinions with close reference to the text.

9

How far do you agree that Miller's exploration of family relationships in *Death of a Salesman* can best be understood in Freudian terms? You should include relevant contextual factors and ideas from your critical reading to support your answer.

 Activity 5

Work through the following steps for each of the questions in the list on page 106 and above.

a) Study the questions and highlight the key words.

b) Plan your answer.

c) Look for quotations to support your planned response.

d) Identify any critical ideas that are relevant to the question and learn some quotations from the critics' own arguments.

Extract-based questions

1

> Starting with the opening of Act Two up to Willy's line 'Beyond a question. G'bye I'm late', analyse the ways in which Miller presents a shift in tone from Act One. Support your answer with close reference to the text.

2

> With close reference to the extract, explore the sequence of action where Biff surprises his father in his hotel room in Boston. You should particularly examine the ways in which Miller reveals Willy's attitudes towards each of the other characters.
>
> The extract begins with the stage direction, '*The* WOMAN *enters laughing*, WILLY *follows her; she is in a black slip*' and ends with Willy's line to Biff, 'Come back here! I'll whip you!'

Tips for assessment

Aim to leave five minutes at the end of your allotted time for answering the question to go back through your work, asking yourself the following questions (and being prepared to put things right):

- Have you written a clear introduction that signals to the examiner that you are answering the specific demands of the question?
- Do you return to the terms of the question regularly enough in your answer?
- Have you used separate paragraphs for each stage of your argument? Does your argument build to a convincing conclusion?
- Have you embedded appropriate quotations into your answer to support your ideas?
- Have you used an appropriate method of linking ideas?
- Have you referred relevantly to the play's context?
- Have you referred relevantly to critics' views?
- Have you used correct terminology, such as: tragedy, expressionism, dialogue, sociolect, semantic field, stage directions, symbolism, characterization?
- Have you checked that your spelling, grammar and punctuation are correct?

Sample answers

Extract from sample answer 1

How does Miller present the theme of memory in *Death of a Salesman*?

This is a purposeful opening to the answer, which shows the student engaging directly with the focus of the question.

Death of a Salesman is written in the genre of a memory play and this is one of the first ways that Miller alerts the audience to the theme of memory. Unlike Tennessee William's memory play, The Glass Menagerie, Miller does not use a narrator figure to point out where the action stems from Willy Loman's memories or when the action represents the unfolding events of the here and now. Instead, the audience is expected to recognize where Willy's memories overcrowd him and he becomes completely absorbed in a past experience.

Miller uses the tools of his trade as a dramatist to clarify those sections of text that recall the past and those that maintain the fiction of an unfolding present. He uses lighting as well as musical motifs to indicate, for example, when the happy days with the boys are absorbing Willy or when the fantastical figure of his dead brother Ben is about to materialize. For

Quotations are used well to support the emerging argument.

example, after Willy's traumatic interview with Howard in Act Two, as Willy 'stares into space, exhausted' the audience hear Ben's theme tune, 'Now the music is heard – BEN's music – first distantly, then closer, closer'. No sooner is Ben gone, reminding Willy of how he could walk out of a new continent 'rich', than another melody is heard, this time 'The gay music of the boys is heard', so we know we are about to go back in time, on this occasion to just before Biff leaves for his big game at Ebbets field. Thus, Miller uses non-diegetic sound (sound where the source is not present on stage), as well as stage effects such as Willy rushing 'through the wall-line of the kitchen and out into the living-room' to present the theme of memory.

Furthermore, the whole of the substance of the plot is based on Willy's, often romanticized but sometimes starkly disturbing, memories of the past. Through these memories, Miller allows the audience to piece together the back-story behind the tense relationship between Biff and Willy, just as he allows us to see the promise in young Biff that has been destroyed by his discovery that his father is 'a phony little fake'. Cleverly, Miller does

This is an interesting section about Miller's ordering of the memories though there is scope for further specific detail.

not reveal the memories in chronological order, for that would be too simple and dramatically uninteresting. Instead he weaves in snippets from when the boys were in their young teens with visitations from Willy's dead brother Ben to create a prism-like effect of past experiences and dreams, all affecting Willy and his mercurial moods in the present-day scenes.

Another method Miller uses to present the theme of memory is to include some characters who only exist in Willy's memory/mind. These characters are Ben and the Woman. Miller first introduces Ben into the play when Willy and Charley are playing cards. Willy's memory of Ben appears to have been jogged by the receipt of a letter from Ben's wife, announcing Ben's death and, even before Charley's entrance, Willy has been voicing his regret that he didn't 'go to Alaska with my brother, Ben that time!' At this stage, we have only seen Willy as an ordinary man in his early sixties, who is exhausted. His reference to Ben appears to be a casual if heartfelt remark. However, Miller then produces Ben as if he has been summoned by Willy's despair and he materializes before us 'with an aura of far places about him'. When Willy is suddenly reminded of Ben by Charley, we hear the first strains of 'Ben's music' and Miller cleverly introduces Ben into a conversation with Willy while Charley is also talking to Willy. The effect on stage is remarkable. Willy can see Ben, but Charley cannot. Ben ignores Charley and yet some of the lines of the conversation would make sense to Charley, while some would not. This is a clever way of presenting the way in which memories take hold of Willy when he is least expecting them.

The other character that only exists in Willy's memory is the Woman, deliberately nameless. We wonder, as an audience, whether Willy has obliterated her name from his memory or whether she signifies a string of fairly anonymous women with whom Willy has had casual affairs over his 30-plus years on the road away from Linda all week. In a Freudian reading of the play, Willy's inability or refusal to name the Woman in his memory is an aspect of his mind's control over his conscious state. His unconscious blocks the memory of his infidelity and he regresses into other moments from his past to avoid confronting the consequences of the memory that he is blocking. The Woman appears several times in the play as the sound of laughter only, here Miller uses diegetic sound to trouble Willy and the audience, offering an ironic 'commentary' on Willy's claim to value Linda as 'the best there is' and making the audience question Linda's assertion that 'few men are idolized by their children the way you are'.

Another method that Miller employs to present the theme of memory is through his use of repeated reference to remembering. In the early sequences of the play Willy is reminiscing about Biff, as he does throughout, asking Linda, 'Remember how they used to follow him around in high school?' Later Willy asks Ben to remind him about his father and Ben replies, 'Well, I don't know how much you remember' before telling him all about his father's adventures selling home-crafted flutes.

Some useful analysis of the way that Miller introduces Ben but textual quotation would further support the point.

More use of quotation to support the developing argument, but the language is not always unpicked carefully enough.

Good focus on language, which is further developed in the full answer.

This is a well-structured and focused extract from an assured student's answer, which goes on to deal with a wider range of techniques. An appreciation of Miller's dramatic methods is very clearly communicated. Appropriate attention is paid to a range of approaches to the theme of memory and the answer is well supported from the text.

Extract from sample answer 2

Miller is often accused of presenting the women in *Death of a Salesman* through the 'male gaze' of Willy Loman. Explore Miller's reasons for presenting the women in the play as he does.

It is certainly true that Miller presents the women in the play through the 'male gaze' of Willy Loman, since Willy is the character whose memories dominate the play and, of course, he is bound to see his wife Linda through a male gaze because he is male.

The focus of the question is clearly targeted but there is scope for further development as the answer proceeds

One of the interesting things about Willy's perspective, however, is that it transforms Linda from the occasionally opinionated character that we see in the scenes set in the present into a more passive and obliging character when filtered through Willy's memory. For example, when Linda contradicts Willy mildly in Act One about there not being 'more people', Willy flies into a rage insisting, 'There's more people! That's what's ruining this country! Population is getting out of control. The competition is maddening!' No such events occur in Willy's memories, as he is able to rearrange events to conform to his ideal of Linda as a helpmate and pal. In the scenes of memory, Linda appears in an idealized form, never opposing Willy's opinions and always happy to flatter him and massage his ego.

This seems like a good point, although there may be some exceptions that would be considered in a stronger answer.

Another point worth making about Miller's presentation of women is that, of course, we are viewing a construct of femininity that belongs to the 1940s through the lens of the 21st century and we cannot help but be shocked by Linda's acceptance of her life of drudgery and subjugation. Not only is Linda depicted as a second-class citizen in the Loman household, waxing floors, taking off Willy's shoes, mending his jacket and her own stockings, while Willy takes brand new stockings to his lover; she is not even included in the celebratory dinner that is planned at the Chop House. Linda does not seem to resent this exclusion; indeed, she accepts it as perfectly normal.

Valid point, but the student misses the opportunity to engage with feminist criticism.

Willy's male gaze sees Linda as much as a mother figure as a wife. She sings him to sleep and makes sure he has got his glasses and handkerchief before going to see Howard much as a mother would with a schoolboy.

In his memory, Willy also remembers the Woman, very much as a sex object. The Woman does not have to mend her stockings as she has Willy to supply her; 'I love a lot of stockings' she says, implying almost that she has more than she needs. The Woman, though described in the stage directions as 'Quite proper-looking, Willy's age' is nevertheless in a man's hotel room at two in the morning and she tolerates, even if she does not enjoy, having her bottom slapped and being kissed 'roughly'. Willy's memory is a guilty one but he still paints himself within it as someone that women like, someone who makes them laugh and someone who has been promised an open door in the store where the Woman works to see the buyers. Miller uses Willy's gaze, in fact, to distort events rather than merely to represent a male viewpoint.

Quotation is used well to support the emerging argument.

Another point worth making is that Willy's male gaze only operates in the memory scenes and that, in the scenes that take place in the present, we see characters through Miller's eyes. In the real-time scenes, Linda is fiercely defensive of Willy to her boys; she is sarcastic with her grown-up sons about how little they have done to help their father and she repeatedly calls them by derogatory names. She tells Happy that he is a 'philandering bum' and Biff that he is no more than a 'boy'. She chastizes Biff for acting like a bird, hopping home when the fancy takes him and she calls them both 'animals' for their abandonment of Willy in the restaurant. Miller shows us a strong woman in Linda, who is prepared to lose her sons to protect her husband, telling them to 'Get out of here, both of you, and don't come back. I don't want you tormenting him any more'.

This is an interesting and well-supported section on Miller's presentation of Linda, although it could analyse the quotation.

In his depiction of Miss Forsythe and the even less significant Letta, Miller presents two young women of 'easy virtue' to make a point about Happy in particular, but about both Willy's sons in general. These two girls are easily picked up by total strangers. Miss Forsythe's posing as a cover girl for 'a lot of' unspecified magazines suggests that she may be as economical with the truth as Happy Loman. In some ways, Miller is suggesting perhaps that such people deserve one another, but it is another poor reflection upon Hap's upbringing that, with the ideal of a wife like Linda in his head, he still chooses girls like the Woman, and women who are engaged and therefore not strictly available, every time. It remains a male gaze, nevertheless.

There is scope for more analysis here; the example is relevant but requires further detailed comment, especially in relation to male stereotypes of women as madonnas or whores.

This answer is relevant to the question and the student makes valid points about the way in which Miller's presentation of women is filtered through Willy's perspective in the memory scenes but without that 'filter' in the scenes depicting the present. Opportunities to engage with feminist criticism of the play have not been taken. Points are made but not always developed.

Extract from sample answer 3

> Starting with the opening of Act Two up to Willy's line 'Beyond a question. G'bye I'm late', analyse the ways in which Miller presents a shift in tone from Act One. Support your answer with close reference to the text.

A clear start that links to the question by describing the tone and contrasts it to the tone at the end of Act One.

A useful comparison is made here; some additional precise detail would improve this comment.

Evidence of close reading but more could be said about the symbolism of the seeds, which Willy plants later on.

The opening of Act Two is significant for its optimistic tone. Unlike some sections in Act One, where Willy was drawn into his own dream-world or where he snapped at Linda or sniped at Biff, at the beginning of Act Two he appears relaxed. Miller signals this change through the stage direction, 'Music is heard, gay and bright'. Previously such music has heralded the arrival of one of Willy's memories about the boys' teenage years but not so here. Here Willy remains in his right mind and considers the prospects of the boys in a positive way.

In Act Two, Willy appears refreshed. He speaks of having slept well for the 'First time in months'. Unlike the beginning of Act One, he uses positive vocabulary, praising Linda for seeing the boys off early, 'Good work' and using the term 'nice and early'. The stage directions tell us that Willy is 'smiling' and he responds to Linda's enthusiasm about the boys with equal enthusiasm. When he tells Linda, 'He's heading for a change. There's no question, there simply are certain men that take longer to get – solidified', the word 'change' and the emphasis of 'no question' show a new mood of optimism that we have only heard before in Willy's happy memories of the boys' teenage years. Willy's optimism is confirmed by his repetition of the phrase, 'There's no question, no question at all' and he is encouraged enough to consider buying seeds on his way home. The relevance of seeds is important as they signify new life and the possibility of a return to the happy life they enjoyed before the apartment buildings blocked out their light. It can even be compared to a return to the Garden of Eden, having been ejected from it, following the discovery of his sin of adultery with the Woman.

Willy's mind then takes a leap into an imagined future, 'You wait, kid, before it's all over we're gonna get a little place out in the country, and I'll raise some vegetables, a couple of chickens...', which again signals a tonal shift from Willy's previous obsession with the past and with the opinions of his dead brother Ben. Instead of bemoaning the fact that the boys have left home, in this opening of Act Two, Willy looks forward with relish to a time when they will visit Willy and Linda in their new abode in the country: 'And they'll get married, and come for a weekend. I'd build a little guest house. 'Cause I got so many fine tools, all I'd need would be a little lumber and some peace of mind.' Here Miller shows Willy revelling in his talent for building and his collection of tools and even anticipating having peace of mind, something that was in short supply in the Act One.

There is scope for developing this point.

The optimism is dented a little once Linda begins to talk about how much ⟵ Shows wider knowledge
money they need to pay their regular bills. As in the rest of the play, she   of the play as well as a
knows the precise amounts of all of their little debts, 'A hundred and eight,   focus on language.
sixty-eight. Because we're a little short again'. We now begin to see Willy
losing a little of his enthusiasm, not snapping exactly, but questioning
Linda again, 'Why are we short?' with some ill-concealed alarm.

Nevertheless, this is short-lived and Willy manages something like a sense
of achievement when Linda announces that they have only one payment
left to make on their mortgage to pay it off. He agrees with Linda when
she describes this as an 'accomplishment'. Willy's cheerfulness reaches new
heights when Linda tells him about the meal that the boys are going to
treat him to. Miller gives him the reactions of a teenage boy rather than a
60-plus year old, as he lapses into the idiolect of a youngster, exclaiming,   Gives a personal
'Gee whiz! That's really somethin'. I'm gonna knock Howard for a loop, kid.   response, but this
I'll get an advance, and I'll come home with a New York job. Goddammit,   ⟵ requires more analysis
now I'm gonna do it!' For anyone who knows how this celebratory meal   of the given extract.
turns out, this is a heart-wrenching moment.

This is a competent analysis of some of Miller's methods with relevant attention
paid to language choice and tone. The student makes some valid comparisons and
effective contrasts between how Willy was presented in Act One and how Miller
presents him in the given extract. Quotations are used carefully to support the ideas.

Extract from sample answer 4

Do you consider Miller's *Death of a Salesman* to have been inspired by Greek tragic models? Support your answer by reference to Miller's play and at least **one** other tragedy that you have considered.

Clear, direct response to the focus of the question.

I agree with those who recognise Death of a Salesman as a form of tragedy that originated with the Greeks, but that has been modified over time.

Reveals relevant knowledge about one of the most important models of tragedy.

Some of Miller's inspirations are in Sophocles' tragedy Oedipus Rex. In this play, the tragic hero Oedipus, King of Thebes, finally confronts his past when he realizes that he was responsible for killing his father (who he did not know) at a place where three roads meet. The realization that he has killed his father and married his mother, a fate predicted for him by the Oracle of Apollo, propels him towards his tragedy. He blinds himself and spends the rest of his life wandering as a beggar.

This interesting parallel demonstrates close consideration of the similarities.

What strikes me most about the similarities between Willy Loman and Oedipus is the way in which their fates were sealed at a particular time and place in their pasts. For Oedipus, the place was a road where three roads meet, where the road from Thebes forks to Daulia and Delphi, where he killed his father and doomed himself. For Willy Loman, the crossroads of his life occurred in Boston where his life converged with his son's, with disastrous results for both of them, in a hotel room, when Willy ceased to be the much-loved father to Biff. For Biff, after the discovery of the Woman,

Quite a sophisticated (and developed) point, which is relevant to the question.

Willy effectively became dead to him; Biff also buried his own future and gave up on life. As Bernard tells Willy, 'I've often thought of how strange it was that I knew he'd given up his life. What happened in Boston, Willy?' In

These are all fair points, taking the argument forward.

both plays, the accidental meeting of father and son triggered the tragic outcome. In both, the discovery of the cause of their tragedy only strikes the protagonist years after the event. In both plays, the heroes are blind to their situation, suggesting that Miller was inspired by the earlier play.

Makes a useful link between the plays.

Willy's blindness is only metaphorical (and a wilful suppression of the truth). He repeatedly tells Linda, 'I won't have you mending stockings in this house' because he does not want to see this reminder of his adultery. Oedipus's blindness, once metaphorical like Willy's, becomes real at the end of the play, when his wife/mother Jocasta commits suicide and Oedipus blinds himself because he cannot bear to see the truth any more. Even the phrase 'wife/mother', used of Jocasta, causes us to consider Linda.

Makes an assertion, but based on a clear example.

Linda, who sings Willy to sleep to soothe him, who checks that he has his handkerchief and glasses before going to see Howard and who protects him fiercely, even against her real sons, reminds us a little of the motherly wife in the Oedipus myth. These similarities suggest that Miller was returning to the Greek tragedy that he loved.

Of course, the story that Miller tells is very different from Sophocles' *Oedipus Rex*. Greek tragedy traditionally dealt with nobility and not with ordinary characters, but Miller argued in his essay, 'Tragedy and the Common Man' (1949), that modern tragedy cannot deal with such figures because the social conditions that existed when Aristotle was writing no longer exist. Miller wrote, 'we no longer live in an era dominated by kings and queens – and so maybe our definition of tragedy should change, too'.

Like Miller's play, Sophocles' tragic trilogy *Antigone*, *Oedipus Rex* and *Oedipus at Colonus* also deals with a family, the family of King Laius, a family cursed for several generations by Apollo. Because it is the family of the head of state, the state inevitably suffers as a result of the family's downfall. One of Aristotle's expectations of tragedy is that it involves the wider state in its implications. Some critics think this is a stumbling block to seeing *Death of a Salesman* as a tragedy inspired by Greek models, but I do not. Willy Loman is not a head of state and his downfall does not implicate the wider state (although it devastates his family). However, it is possible to see Willy Loman as a figurehead for the ordinary family man. It is possible to see, in the American god Consumerism, something of the vengeful god Apollo and it is possible to see Willy Loman, like Oedipus, as both tragic hero and tragic victim of a fate that he could not escape because it was decreed at his birth. As Charley says, at the end of the Requiem, 'Nobody dast blame this man. A salesman is got to dream, boy. It comes with the territory'. The implication, in the full speech, is that Willy was born to be a salesman and was in some way doomed to fail.

Refers to the question again and states a clear view.

Attempts a useful comparison between the forces operating in Sophocles' time and those in Miller's.

Uses useful quotation to support the point made above.

Let us consider some of the other tenets of Aristotelian tragedy that can be seen operating in Miller's play. The play follows the inevitable progress toward death of the flawed protagonist, who, through his memories and fractured mental state, gains a growing self-awareness. The plot concerns a single story, of some seriousness, without subplots and with a clear beginning, middle and end. Miller retains – in the real-time scenes, at least – a unity of time and place, as well as of action. Most importantly, it is a play that draws the audience in and the audience responds with both pity and fear.

Offers a thoughtful development of the argument and returns to tenets of Aristotelian tragedy.

Shows secure knowledge of Aristotelian model.

The critic Dan Vogel, in an article entitled 'Willy Tyrannos' (1974), comments that both Willy and Oedipus search for the truth while simultaneously fearing it. Certainly Willy refuses to acknowledge the reasons for the rift with Biff, deflecting Linda's question at the end of Act One, when she asks point blank, 'Willy dear, what has he got against you?', by retorting, 'I'm so tired. Don't talk any more'. Vogel also suggests that, while Willy's earlier suicide

Cites the ideas of a relevant critic, summarized succinctly, and exemplifies with quotations.

attempts were the result of his despair, his death is actually borne out of his epiphany that Biff truly loves him and therefore that his death, like those of Greek heroes, is sacrificial and life-affirming. He tells Ben, 'Loves me. [Wonderingly.] Always loved me. Isn't that a remarkable thing? Ben, he'll worship me for it!'

The close of the play is not merely cathartic in the Greek tragic mode, it is deeply moving. Just as happens at the end of Shakespeare's *King Lear*, the 'foolish, fond old man' Lear, is finally reunited with his favourite child Cordelia, whom he had banished for not declaring her love for him. Like Willy, Lear has become deranged, accepting that 'I am not in my perfect mind' but he is still able to recognize Cordelia and finally to accept that she has always loved him. Lear dies, secure in that knowledge, as Willy does in Miller's tragedy, speaking almost his final words to the teenage boy that he worshipped and who once worshipped him in return, 'when you hit, hit low and hit hard, because it's important, boy'.

> Moves seamlessly from Greek to Shakespearean models of tragedy.

This is a personal approach to the question, exploring similarities between *Death of a Salesman* and *Oedipus Rex* as well as some of Aristotle's prescriptions about tragedy. It includes some purposeful reference to Miller's own comments about tragedy and to another critic's views. The later part of the answer begins to consider Miller's debt to *King Lear*. Well-structured, this answer uses specialist terminology with confidence, is fluently argued and well supported.

Glossary

antithesis a direct opposite or contrast

antonym a word that has the opposite meaning to another word, e.g. 'big', 'little'

backchannel little words or sounds made in conversation that do not interrupt the speaker but acknowledge that the listener is listening

catastrophe in Greek tragedy, the concluding part of the play where the protagonist accepts ruin

catharsis the intended audience experience at the end of the tragedy, purging them of the twin emotions of pity and fear

classical allusion figurative language that compares events or characters from the classical world of myth to modern parallels

climax the highest or most intense part of the play

complication or reversal conflicts or problems that threaten or reverse the protagonist's progress

denouement the resolution of the plot

ellipses the row of dots on a page of text that indicate a pause or trailing away in a train of thought and/or speech

exclamation a word used to express surprise or shock or a strong emotion about something; the type of phrase or clause associated with exclamations is called exclamative

exposition introduction of key information about setting, characters and situation to help the audience make sense of the play

expressionism a form of theatre that originated in Germany in the early 20th century in which characters' inner feelings and/or thoughts are expressed outwardly in a form of physical expression or represented through concrete staging elements such as setting, lighting and/or sound

external structure the physical shape of a piece of literature, determined by the way its content is arranged and presented by the writer

figurative language language that uses figures of speech, is metaphorical and not literal

foil in literature, a character whose characteristics completely contrast with one of the main characters, highlighting the character traits of that main character

hackneyed platitude an expression such as a cliché, which is unimaginative and commonplace

hyperbole a form of overstatement or exaggeration

impressionistic language that creates personal ideas and impressions rather than literal facts

improvisation in theatre, the creation of dramatic scenes without written dialogue and with no predetermined scenario; actors draw on their own imaginations to create episodes of action either to generate original drama or to explore aspects of given characters

internal structure the sequencing of events in a piece of literature, whether chronologically or otherwise

leitmotif a musical phrase or melody associated with specific characters or ideas and repeated in the course of a performance

lexis the linguistic term for words, terms, expression

meta-theatre a form of theatre that draws attention to its own theatricality, e.g. when a narrator or Chorus figure steps outside the action to address the audience

method acting a painstaking approach to acting based on a system evolved by Constantin Stanislavski in the early 20th century; in essence, it provides actors with methods for recalling and utilizing aspects of their own character and experiences to create a role

motif   a word, phrase, image, idea or sound used in literature that is repeated and builds up a resonance through its repeated patterning; in *Death of a Salesman*, motifs include references to time, repeated phrases such as 'being well liked', references to the woods, forests, or the jungle, to the silk stockings, etc.

non-linear structure   a plot that does not proceed chronologically

non-sequitur   a statement (or a response) that does not follow logically from or is not clearly related to anything previously said

personification   a device whereby a writer assigns qualities of a living person to inanimate objects

prop   a moveable object used on stage by the actors

proscenium arch   the often arched structure over the stage that is part of the structure of the theatre and not part of the stage set

protagonist   the main character

realism   a genre of literature that attempts to create a faithful representation of life

refrain   in music, a repeated melody or tune

requiem   a religious service, piece of music or poem designed to honour the dead

revolve stage   a stage with a large circular area that can be rotated either as part of the action or to reveal new settings

script   the written version of the play as used in rehearsals for a performance

semantic field   a group of words connected by a shared field of reference, e.g. words associated with light and darkness or with nature

semantics   in linguistics, refers to the study of meaning

social milieu   the physical environment and social class of the characters who inhabit it

social realism   a genre that adopts a realistic approach and focuses on everyday life; usually on the working classes, the poor or the destitute, the work encompasses a critique of dominant social structures

socialism   an ideology based on the belief that society should be run on egalitarian principles, e.g. with cooperative ownership of businesses, where profits are shared amongst all the people involved

sociolect   a language style associated with a particular social group; the 'style' includes use of grammatical construction, choice of **lexis** and deployment of **semantic fields**

symbol   an object that represents or extends deeper implications about character or situation than may be suggested by their surface appearance

tableau   a brief scene when the actors are seen quite still, without moving, on stage

tragic flaw (hamartia)   a character fault that leads to the hero's downfall

tragic hero   the main character, who falls from greatness to misery because of a character flaw

tragic recognition (anagnorisis)   recognition that the tragedy has been self-inflicted

transposition   in theatre, the creation of a production set in a completely different time period or geographical setting from the original; some plays lend themselves more readily to transposition than others

vernacular speech   a language or dialect that is native to a particular region or country rather than to a literary or cultured language

OXFORD
UNIVERSITY PRESS

Great Clarendon Street, Oxford, OX2 6DP, United Kingdom

Oxford University Press is a department of the University of Oxford. It furthers the
University's objective of excellence in research, scholarship, and education by publishing
worldwide. Oxford is a registered trade mark of Oxford University Press in the UK and in
certain other countries

British Library Cataloguing in Publication Data

Data available

ISBN 978-019-839902-5

Kindle edition ISBN 978-019-839903-2

10 9 8 7 6 5 4 3 2 1

Printed in China by Leo Paper Products

Acknowledgements
The publisher and authors would like to thank the following for permission to use
photographs and other copyright material:

Cover: Cultura RM/Alamy Stock Photo; **p7:** Geraint Lewis/Alamy Stock Photo; **p12:**
Columbia/REX/Shutterstock; **p18:** Alastair Muir/REX/Shutterstock; **p22:** Everett Collection
Inc/Alamy Stock Photo; **p24:** W. Eugene Smith/Getty Images; **p29:** Granger Historical
Picture Archive/Alamy Stock Photo; **p35:** REUTERS/Alamy Stock Photo; **p43:** Geraint Lewis/
Alamy Stock Photo; **p50, 56:** Photostage; **p59:** Photo by Ellie Kurttz © RSC; **p65:** Everett
Collection Inc/Alamy Stock Photo; **p69:** Moviestore collection Ltd/Alamy Stock Photo; **p74:**
ClassicStock/Alamy Stock Photo; **p78:** Moviestore collection Ltd/Alamy Stock Photo; **p80:**
Alastair Muir/REX/Shutterstock; **p86:** Everett Collection Inc/Alamy Stock Photo; **p87:**
Eileen Darby; **p89:** Photo by Ellie Kurttz © RSC; **p96, 100:** Everett Collection Inc/Alamy
Stock Photo.

Every effort has been made to contact copyright holders of material reproduced in this
book. Any omissions will be rectified in subsequent printings if notice is given to the
publisher.

We are grateful for permission to reprint the following copyright texts:

Extracts from *Death of a Salesman* by Arthur Miller (Penguin Modern Classics, 2000),
copyright © Arthur Miller 1949, 1977, reprinted by permission of The Wylie Agency (UK)
Ltd. All rights reserved.

Arthur Miller: extracts from 'Tragedy and the Common Man', 'On Social Plays', 'The Family
in Modern Drama' and 'Introduction to the *Collected Plays*' in *The Theatre Essays of Arthur
Miller* edited by Robert A Martin (Methuen, 1978), copyright © Arthur Miller 1978, reprinted
by permission of The Wylie Agency (UK) Ltd. All rights reserved.

Raymond Williams: extract from *Drama from Ibsen to Brecht* (Chatto & Windus, 1968),
reprinted by permission of The Random House Group Ltd.

Tennessee Williams: extracts from *The Glass Menagerie*, copyright © 1945, renewed 1973
by The University of the South, reprinted by permission of Georges Borchardt, Inc, for the
Estate of Tennessee Williams. All rights reserved.

We have made every effort to trace and contact copyright holders before publication.
If notified, the publisher will rectify any errors or omissions at the earliest opportunity.